Executive Strategies for Agile Software Engineering and Architecture

Suji Daniel-Paul

1

Table of Contents

Preface

Introduction

Welcome to "Executive Strategies for Agile Software Engineering and Architecture," a book designed to bridge the practical world of Agile methodologies with the strategic thinking required at the executive level. This book is aimed at leaders, managers, and aspiring executives within the fields of software engineering and architecture who are eager to integrate Agile practices into their leadership and project management approaches.

Author's Background

My journey into the worlds of software development and architectural design has spanned over a decade, during which I have held roles ranging from developer to senior executive. Throughout my career, I have witnessed first-hand the transformational impact that Agile methodologies can have on projects, teams, and entire organizations. This experience has fueled my passion for Agile practices and inspired me to write this book—to share the insights and strategies that have been most effective in my professional life.

The Importance of Agile in Modern Leadership

The landscape of technology and business is evolving at an unprecedented pace, driven by rapid advancements in technology and changing market demands. Traditional project management methodologies are often ill-equipped to handle this rate of change, leading to delays, cost overruns, and missed opportunities. Agile methodologies, with their emphasis on flexibility, responsiveness, and collaboration, offer a powerful alternative. By adopting Agile practices, leaders can ensure their teams are more adaptable, more efficient, and more attuned to the needs of their customers.

Overview of Agile Principles

Agile is nor merely a buzzword, but a set of principles and practices that fundamentally change how projects are managed. At its core, Agile is about iterative development, continuous feedback, and high adaptability. Unlike traditional methods, which often require extensive upfront planning and rigid execution frameworks, Agile allows teams to adjust their strategies as projects evolve, responding quickly to challenges and opportunities as they arise.

Scope of the Book

This book is structured to walk you through every aspect of integrating Agile into high-level management and strategic planning. Each chapter explores different facets of Agile leadership, from setting up Agile teams and managing complex software projects to fostering an Agile culture across multiple departments. The book combines theoretical frameworks with practical advice, enriched by case studies from leading companies that have successfully embraced Agile methodologies.

Methodology and Research

The insights in this book are grounded in both extensive research and personal experience. I have conducted numerous interviews with industry leaders who have led Agile transformations, surveyed hundreds of Agile practitioners, and analyzed several case studies of successful Agile implementations. The methodologies and strategies discussed are those that have proven effective across various industries and organizational sizes.

Personal Reflections

Writing this book has been both a challenge and a profound learning experience. One of the biggest challenges was distilling a wide range of Agile practices and leadership strategies into actionable advice that executives can realistically implement. My aim has been to present this information in a way that is both accessible and engaging, providing a clear path for readers to follow in their own Agile journeys.

Acknowledgments

I am deeply grateful to a number of people who have contributed to the creation of this book. My colleagues, both past and present, provided invaluable insights and feedback. I would also like to thank the many Agile coaches and consultants whose work has informed much of the content presented here.

Closing Thoughts

As we look to the future, the role of Agile leadership in software engineering and architecture is only set to grow. This book is intended not just as a guide, but as a starting point for your exploration into Agile leadership. I encourage you to adapt the principles and strategies discussed to fit your unique circumstances and to continue learning and adapting as you go. I invite you to engage with the content, apply it in your work, and share your experiences with Agile methodologies.

Chapter 1: Introduction to Agile Leadership

Faced by rapid technological advancements, shifting market demands, and an ever-evolving competitive landscape, organizations are under unprecedented pressure to adapt quickly and deliver value consistently. Agile methodologies have emerged as a transformative approach to managing this complexity, enabling teams to respond to change with speed and precision. However, the success of Agile extends beyond frameworks and processes—it requires strong, visionary leadership.

Agile leadership is the cornerstone of successful Agile transformations. It is a leadership style that empowers teams, fosters collaboration, and champions adaptability across all levels of an organization. Unlike traditional command-and-control models, Agile leadership is about creating environments where innovation thrives, decisions are decentralized, and teams are equipped to navigate uncertainty with confidence.

This chapter sets the stage for understanding the role of leadership in fostering an Agile mindset. We will explore the foundational principles of Agile leadership, the unique challenges leaders face in Agile environments, and the key competencies required to inspire and guide teams through change. By understanding these concepts, leaders can position themselves to drive impactful Agile transformations that not only meet business objectives but also create a culture of resilience and continuous improvement.

Understanding Agile Leadership

Definition and Importance

Agile leadership is a management approach that embodies the principles and practices of Agile methodologies to enhance responsiveness to change, promote flexibility, and encourage a collaborative work environment. This leadership style is particularly important in fields like software engineering and architecture, where projects can be complex and environments rapidly changing. Agile leaders focus on enabling their teams to iterate work processes quickly in response to feedback and changes in project scope or objectives. This leadership style is not just about managing tasks; it's about inspiring and facilitating a culture that embraces change, values experimentation, and prioritizes customer satisfaction.

Core Principles of Agile Leadership

Agile leadership is grounded in several core principles that distinguish it from more traditional leadership approaches:

- **Flexibility in Decision-Making**: Unlike traditional leadership, which often relies on hierarchical, top-down decision-making, Agile leadership values a more collaborative and flexible approach. Decisions are made based on real-time data and team feedback, allowing for quicker adjustments that better meet project needs and customer demands.

- **Empowerment of Teams**: Agile leaders empower their teams by delegating authority and encouraging autonomy. This empowerment allows team members to own their work and make decisions that affect their tasks directly, which can lead to higher engagement and productivity.

- **Commitment to Continuous Improvement**: Continuous improvement is a staple of Agile methodology. Agile leaders commit themselves and their teams to ongoing learning and development, constantly seeking ways to do things better, streamline processes, and innovate solutions.

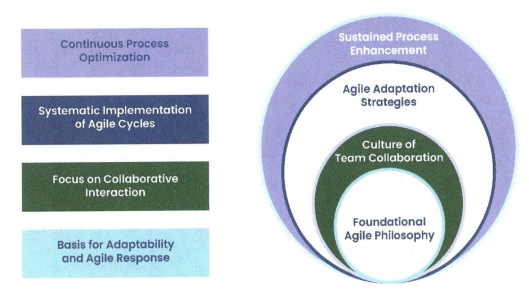

Figure: The Core Components of Agile Leadership

Agile leadership requires a balance between foundational principles and practical strategies that drive collaboration and continuous improvement. The diagram above illustrates the key components of Agile leadership, from establishing a foundational Agile philosophy to fostering a culture of collaboration and implementing adaptation strategies. By embracing these elements, leaders can sustain process optimization and enable their organizations to thrive in dynamic environments.

The Agile Mindset

Adopting an Agile mindset is crucial for leaders who wish to effectively implement Agile practices. This mindset involves several shifts:

- **From Command and Control to Empower and Support**: Agile leaders move away from micromanaging, instead facilitating and supporting their teams' efforts to solve problems and achieve goals independently.

- **From Planning Everything Upfront to Adapting as You Go**: While some planning is always necessary, Agile leaders understand the value of adapting plans as work progresses and new information becomes available. This approach is crucial in technology projects where requirements can change rapidly due to external market forces or new insights.

- **From Avoiding Change to Embracing It**: Agile leaders not only accept change but embrace it as an opportunity for growth and improvement. They foster a culture where change is seen as positive and necessary for success.

These foundational concepts of Agile leadership set the stage for deeper exploration into how executives can apply these principles to drive effective management and innovative practices in their organizations. Agile leadership is not a one-size-fits-all solution but a flexible approach that can be tailored to meet the unique challenges and opportunities of software engineering and architecture projects.

Agile Leadership Framework

Framework Components

Agile leadership is structured around a framework that integrates three key components: vision and strategy, people and culture, and processes and tools. Each component plays a crucial role in ensuring that Agile principles are effectively embedded into an organization's DNA.

The Agile Leadership Framework encompasses two core dimensions: adopting a new mindset for Agile effectiveness and implementing operational practices that align with Agile principles. The diagram below illustrates these interconnected dimensions, highlighting key focus areas such as vision alignment, servant leadership, and iterative transformation. This framework provides a comprehensive approach for leaders to drive Agile transformations successfully.

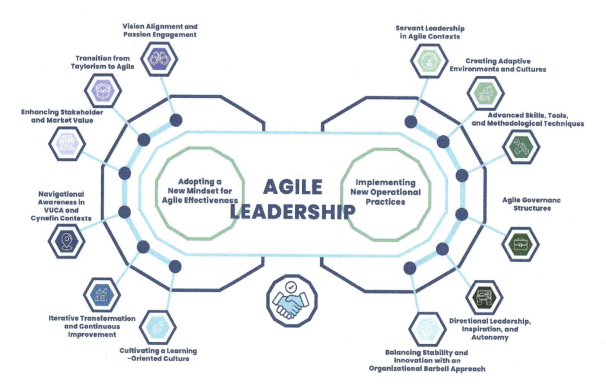

Figure: Agile Leadership Framework

- **Vision and Strategy**: Agile leaders must align their Agile practices with the broader business vision and strategic goals. This alignment ensures that Agile methodologies are not just executed as tactical tools but are integrated into the strategic fabric of the organization. Agile leaders use roadmaps that are flexible and can be adapted as market conditions and organizational priorities evolve. This strategic agility allows the company to remain competitive and responsive to change.

- **People and Culture**: At the heart of Agile leadership is a focus on people and culture. Agile leaders work to cultivate an environment that values collaboration, transparency, and openness. They promote a culture where feedback is actively sought and valued, mistakes are viewed as learning opportunities, and continuous improvement is a collective goal. This cultural shift can be challenging but is essential for Agile practices to take root and flourish.

- **Processes and Tools**: Effective Agile leadership requires the adoption of processes and tools that support Agile methodologies. This includes implementing frameworks like Scrum, Kanban, or Lean, which help structure how work is managed and executed. Additionally, Agile leaders promote the use of tools that enhance collaboration and transparency, such as Agile project management software, real-time communication platforms, and shared dashboards that track project progress and metrics.

Implementing Agile Leadership

Putting Agile leadership into practice involves several practical steps that can help executives integrate these principles effectively:

- **Assess Current Practices**: Begin by assessing the current state of project management and leadership practices within the organization. Identify areas where traditional methods prevail and explore opportunities for introducing Agile practices.

- **Educate and Train Leaders**: Agile leadership requires a different set of skills and a new mindset. Providing training and education for leaders and managers is critical to ensure they understand and can effectively implement Agile principles.

- **Pilot Agile Practices**: Start small by piloting Agile practices on a single team or project. This allows leaders to experiment with Agile methodologies, learn from the experience, and understand the practical adjustments needed before rolling out more broadly.

- **Gather Feedback and Adapt**: Use feedback from the pilot projects to refine and adapt the approach. Agile is all about iteration and continuous improvement, and this applies to leadership practices as well.

Case Studies

Tech Giant's Shift to Agile

Company Background:
Imagine a multinational technology firm traditionally known for its hierarchical structure and slow-moving product development processes. Facing increased competition from more agile startups and rapid technology changes, the company recognized the need for a strategic overhaul.

Agile Transformation Journey:
The transformation began with a pilot project in the software development department, spearheaded by the Chief Technology Officer (CTO). The success of this pilot led to a company-wide adoption of Agile methodologies. The initiative focused on shortening

development cycles, enhancing team collaboration, and improving responsiveness to customer feedback.

Executive Leadership Role:
The CTO played a pivotal role, not only advocating for the adoption of Agile practices but also participating in training sessions and daily stand-ups. This hands-on involvement helped bridge the gap between executive leadership and operational teams, demonstrating a commitment to the Agile process.

Challenges and Solutions:
One of the major challenges was resistance from middle management, who were accustomed to traditional command-and-control practices. To address this, the company implemented extensive training programs and established a mentorship system pairing experienced Agile coaches with managers. This facilitated a smoother transition and helped embed Agile values across the organization.

Outcomes and Benefits:
The shift to Agile resulted in a 40% reduction in time to market for new products and a significant increase in employee engagement and customer satisfaction. The iterative approach allowed for quicker adjustments based on user feedback, leading to better-aligned products.

Lessons Learned:
Key takeaways included the importance of executive buy-in for successful Agile transformation and the need for ongoing education and support structures to sustain change.

Retail Corporation's Agile Adoption

Company Background:
Consider a large retail chain struggling to keep up with market demands and facing stiff competition from more technologically adept competitors. The executive team decided to implement Agile to increase operational flexibility and enhance customer responsiveness.

Agile Transformation Journey:
The journey started within the IT department, with the Agile framework later extended to logistics and customer service operations. The CEO endorsed the transformation, ensuring that Agile principles were integrated into all business units.

Executive Leadership Role:
The CEO actively participated in the Agile rollout, including regular reviews and adjustments to business strategies based on Agile reports and outcomes. This top-level involvement ensured that Agile was not viewed just as an IT initiative but as a core business strategy.

Challenges and Solutions:
Integrating Agile into non-IT departments posed significant challenges, particularly in aligning different operational tempos and vocabularies. The solution was to tailor Agile methodologies to fit the unique needs of each department, supported by specialized Agile coaches.

Outcomes and Benefits:
The adoption of Agile practices led to a more adaptable supply chain and improved customer service, with a 30% quicker response time to market changes and customer needs.

Lessons Learned:
The corporation learned that Agile can be adapted beyond software development to enhance overall business agility. The commitment from the top was crucial in fostering a culture that embraces continuous improvement and rapid adaptation.

These case studies demonstrate that Agile transformation can be successful in different sectors and company sizes when executives play an active and supportive role. The lessons learned highlight the necessity of executive leadership in championing Agile principles, ensuring that the transformation is perceived as a strategic initiative vital to the organization's success.

The Role of Executives in Agile Transformation

Leading by Example

One of the most critical aspects of Agile transformation is the example set by those at the top. Executives who embody Agile principles in their leadership style and decision-making processes inspire their teams to adopt these practices. Leading by example involves:

- **Demonstrating Flexibility and Adaptability**: Executives should show their teams that they are willing to adapt their strategies based on team input and changing conditions. This can involve shifting priorities, adjusting project scopes, or experimenting with new approaches in real-time.

- **Openness to Feedback**: A key Agile principle is continuous improvement, which is fueled by regular feedback. Executives should not only encourage their teams to provide feedback but also actively demonstrate how to integrate this feedback into improvements in processes and behaviors.

- **Transparency in Decision-Making**: Keeping communication open and transparent helps to build trust and shows teams that their contributions are valued and considered in the decision-making process.

Challenges and Solutions

Transitioning to Agile leadership can present several challenges, particularly in organizations accustomed to more traditional management styles. Some common challenges include:

- **Resistance to Change**: Change can be difficult, and some team members may be skeptical of Agile methods, especially if they are used to hierarchical, directive leadership.
    - *Solution*: Education and training are essential. Providing clear examples of Agile success and gradually integrating Agile practices can help ease the transition.

- **Managing Distributed Teams**: Agile relies heavily on communication and collaboration, which can be more challenging with remote or distributed teams.
    - *Solution*: Leveraging technology to maintain communication and collaboration is crucial. Regular video calls, collaborative tools, and consistent updates can help maintain the Agile rhythm.

- **Aligning Various Departments**: Sometimes, different departments may operate in silos, which makes it difficult to implement a cohesive Agile strategy across the organization.

o *Solution*: Executives must work to break down silos by fostering interdepartmental collaboration and establishing shared goals and metrics that align with Agile principles.

Tools and Resources

For executives to effectively lead Agile transformations, several tools and resources can prove invaluable. These include:

- **Agile Project Management Software**: Tools like Jira, Asana, and Trello can help manage projects in an Agile environment by facilitating task tracking, progress updates, and team collaboration.

- **Communication Platforms**: Tools such as Slack and Microsoft Teams enable constant communication and quick problem-solving among team members.

- **Agile Coaching and Consultancy**: Sometimes, bringing in external experts to train and coach teams can accelerate the Agile transformation process.

Summary and Conclusions

In this opening chapter, we have laid the foundation for understanding what Agile leadership entails and the pivotal role executives play in fostering an Agile culture within organizations. We've discussed the importance of leading by example, the necessity of embracing a flexible and adaptive leadership style, and how executives can effectively address the common challenges that arise during an Agile transformation.

The chapter highlighted several key aspects:

- The need for executives to embody Agile principles, demonstrating adaptability, openness to feedback, and transparency in their decision-making processes.

- Strategies to overcome obstacles such as resistance to change, difficulties in managing distributed teams, and the challenge of aligning multiple departments under a unified Agile approach.

- The tools and resources that can aid in these endeavors, ranging from Agile project management software to professional Agile coaching.

By embracing the strategies outlined, executives can not only enhance their leadership capabilities but also drive their organizations towards more dynamic, responsive, and collaborative work environments. This transformation goes beyond mere methodology adoption—it's about cultivating an organizational ethos that thrives on continuous improvement and agile response to change.

Chapter 2: Strategic Planning for Technology Projects

In today's fast-paced and ever-changing business environment, long-term plans often become obsolete before they can be fully implemented. Organizations must adapt quickly to shifting market demands, technological disruptions, and competitive pressures to remain relevant. This need for adaptability has given rise to the concept of strategic agility—a critical capability for executives leading technology-intensive fields.

Strategic agility is more than just reacting to change; it is the ability to anticipate trends, make informed decisions rapidly, and align resources to seize emerging opportunities. For executives, this means adopting a mindset that prioritizes flexibility, iterative planning, and the continuous alignment of strategy with reality.

This chapter explores how Agile principles can be applied to strategic decision-making and long-term planning. We will explore frameworks that enhance strategic responsiveness, discuss the role of executive leadership in driving strategic agility, and provide actionable insights for balancing short-term adaptability with long-term vision. By embracing strategic agility, executives can position their organizations to thrive in a world of constant change and uncertainty.

Introduction to Strategic Agility

In today's rapidly evolving business environment, the ability to adapt quickly and effectively to changing market conditions, technological advancements, and global economic shifts is more crucial than ever. Strategic agility represents a core capability for organizations seeking to maintain competitive advantage and responsiveness in such a dynamic context. This chapter introduces the concept of strategic agility, outlining its importance and the fundamental principles that underpin agile strategic planning.

The Evolving Business Landscape

Modern businesses operate in a world where change is the only constant. Innovations disrupt traditional markets overnight, consumer preferences shift with increasing speed, and new competitors emerge from unexpected quarters. In this high-velocity environment, traditional long-term planning models often fall short. They lack the flexibility to pivot quickly in response to unexpected changes, potentially leading organizations to miss out on critical opportunities or to fail to mitigate emerging risks.

Defining Strategic Agility

Strategic agility is the capability of an organization to rapidly reconfigure and realign its strategies and operations to respond to and capitalize on changes in the external environment. It combines the foresight to anticipate market shifts with the operational flexibility to react swiftly and effectively, ensuring that the organization remains aligned with its strategic goals while adapting to new opportunities and challenges.

- **Key Components of Strategic Agility**:
  - **Sensing Changes**: Continuously monitoring the external environment to identify emerging trends, potential disruptions, and subtle shifts in consumer behavior.

- o **Decision Velocity**: Accelerating the decision-making process without sacrificing the quality of decisions, enabling the organization to act quickly.

- o **Resource Fluidity**: The ability to reallocate resources rapidly—be it capital, personnel, or technology—to where they are most needed, without significant bureaucratic hurdles.

Importance of Strategic Agility

Strategic agility is not merely a beneficial attribute but a crucial determinant of an organization's survival and success in the 21st century. Companies that exhibit high levels of strategic agility can not only withstand pressures from market disruptions but can also emerge as leaders and innovators, shaping the directions of their industries.

- **Competitive Advantage**: Agile organizations are often first to market with new innovations and can adapt quickly to undercut competitors' advantages.

- **Resilience**: Strategic agility enhances an organization's resilience, allowing it to navigate crises and adverse conditions more effectively than its peers.

- **Alignment with Modern Workforces**: Today's employees, particularly millennials and Gen Z, prefer working in dynamic and responsive environments. An agile strategic approach helps attract and retain top talent.

As we explore deeper into the components and implementation of strategic agility, it is clear that this approach is not just about staying competitive. It is about redefining how organizations operate, make decisions, and innovate in an interconnected world. The following sections will explore how leaders can cultivate these capabilities within their teams and throughout their organizations, ensuring that agility becomes a core component of their strategic arsenal.

Implementing Strategic Agility

Framework Adaptation and Practical Implementation

To effectively implement strategic agility within an organization, leaders must adapt existing frameworks to accommodate rapid decision-making and flexible strategic execution. This involves revising traditional practices to become more responsive and incorporating agile principles at the strategic level.

The strategic planning process involves structured steps to ensure that projects align with organizational goals while adapting to dynamic market conditions. The diagram below outlines a systematic approach, from environmental assessment to portfolio review, incorporating tools like decision matrices and project evaluation grids. This process ensures strategic alignment, resource optimization, and informed decision-making, which are critical for Agile organizations operating in complex environments.

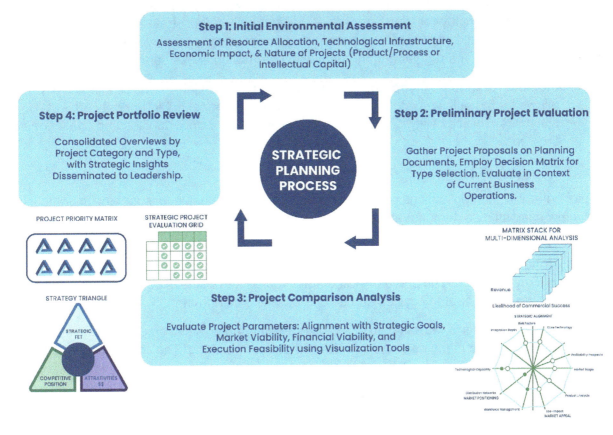

Figure: Agile Strategic Planning Process

Adapting Frameworks for Agility

- **Agile Strategic Planning**: Move away from the traditional annual planning cycle and towards a more dynamic strategic planning process that allows for adjustments on a quarterly or even on-demand basis. This approach ensures that the organization's strategies remain relevant in a fast-changing environment.

- **Scenario Planning**: Integrate scenario planning into strategic reviews to anticipate potential future conditions and prepare multiple strategic responses. This readiness allows the organization to react more swiftly and appropriately as scenarios unfold.

- **Decentralized Decision-Making**: Empower mid-level managers and team leaders to make strategic decisions without waiting for top-level approval. This decentralization speeds up the organization's response times and enhances its ability to capitalize on emerging opportunities.

Implementing Agile Strategic Processes

- **Real-Time Data Utilization**: Leverage real-time data to make informed strategic decisions. Investing in advanced analytics and business intelligence systems can provide leadership with up-to-the-minute insights into market conditions, operational performance, and competitive dynamics.

- **Feedback Loops**: Establish rapid feedback loops with stakeholders, including customers, employees, and partners, to continuously refine strategies based on external input. This could involve more frequent customer surveys, employee feedback mechanisms, and regular engagement with external business partners.

- **Flexible Resource Allocation**: Develop a system for flexible resource allocation that allows for the quick redistribution of budgets and personnel to high-priority projects or initiatives. This flexibility is crucial for responding to new opportunities and challenges as they arise.

Case Studies in Strategic Agility

Exploring real-world applications of strategic agility provides valuable lessons and insights. Here are a few case studies demonstrating successful implementation of strategic agility:

1. **Tech Startup Scaling**: A tech startup rapidly scaled its operations by adopting a flexible strategic framework that allowed it to pivot its business model in response to initial market feedback. The company used agile sprints for business development processes, shortening its strategy cycles and quickly adapting its offerings.

2. **Global Retailer's Market Entry**: A global retailer successfully entered a new market by using scenario planning and decentralized decision-making. The company prepared multiple entry strategies tailored to different potential market conditions, which were quickly executed based on real-time market analysis and local team insights.

3. **Financial Services Innovation**: A financial services firm introduced a new mobile banking service using strategic agility. The firm continuously updated its launch strategy based on ongoing customer feedback and competitive developments, significantly shortening its product development cycle and improving the product-market fit.

Implementing strategic agility involves more than just adopting new tools or processes; it requires a fundamental shift in how an organization thinks about strategy and decision-making. By adopting flexible strategic frameworks, empowering decision-makers at all levels, and leveraging real-time data, organizations can enhance their responsiveness and adaptability. The case studies provided offer concrete examples of how diverse organizations have successfully navigated these changes, leading to substantial competitive advantages and operational improvements.

The strategic planning process illustrated in these cases study aligns with the structured framework depicted below. By employing steps such as environmental analysis, project evaluation, and portfolio assessment, organizations can achieve strategic alignment while optimizing resource allocation. This process ensures informed decision-making and successful implementation of Agile strategies.

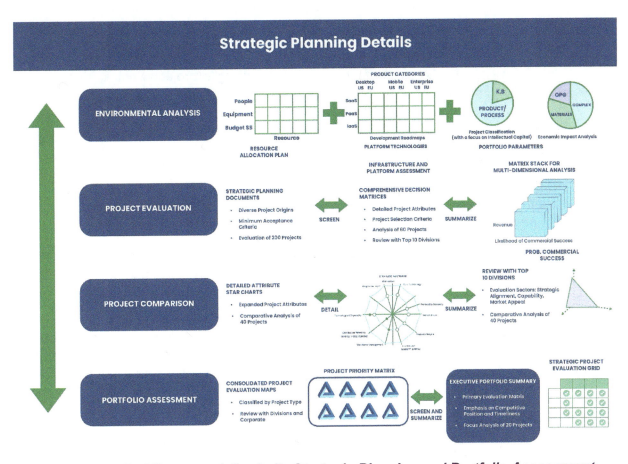

Figure: Detailed Framework for Agile Strategic Planning and Portfolio Assessment

Integrating Enterprise Risk Management with Strategic Agility

Incorporating risk management into strategic agility allows organizations to not only respond quickly to changes but also to anticipate and mitigate potential risks that could impact strategic objectives. This section explores how leaders can effectively intertwine enterprise risk management (ERM) with agile strategic planning to enhance both proactive and reactive capabilities.

Enterprise Risk Management in Agile Contexts

Enterprise risk management traditionally involves identifying, assessing, and preparing for potential losses or dangers that could hinder an organization's operations and objectives. In agile environments, this concept must be adapted to fit the rapid pace and iterative nature of agile methodologies.

- **Agile Risk Identification**: Risk identification in agile settings should be continuous. Agile teams need to develop mechanisms for identifying risks at every stage of the project lifecycle, incorporating tools like automated risk scanning and real-time monitoring systems.

- **Dynamic Risk Assessment**: Unlike traditional static risk assessments conducted at set intervals, dynamic assessments are integrated into the agile workflows. For example, each sprint could include risk assessment as part of the retrospective, allowing teams to evaluate new risks and the effectiveness of mitigation strategies regularly.

- **Risk Prioritization**: Given the fast-paced nature of agile projects, not all risks can be addressed simultaneously. Agile leaders must prioritize risks based on their potential impact on the project's key deliverables and the organization's long-term goals. Techniques such as risk matrices or impact probability charts can be adapted for agile environments to facilitate quicker decision-making.

Strategies for Risk Integration

Merging risk management with agile strategic planning involves several key strategies that ensure both areas enhance each other rather than operate in silos.

- **Embedding Risk Management in Agile Ceremonies**: Incorporate risk discussions into standard agile ceremonies such as sprint planning, daily stand-ups, and sprint reviews. This integration ensures that risk considerations are not an afterthought but a regular part of decision-making processes.

- **Utilizing Technology for Risk Management**: Leverage technology to enhance risk management capabilities. For instance, predictive analytics can forecast potential risks based on historical data, while AI-driven tools can provide scenario analysis to assess the impact of different risk mitigation strategies.

- **Creating Agile Risk Response Teams**: Develop small, cross-functional teams responsible for monitoring and responding to risks as they arise. These teams can act quickly to implement mitigation strategies, ensuring that responses are both timely and effective.

Case Studies: Integrating Enterprise Risk Management with Agile Strategies

The integration of Enterprise Risk Management (ERM) with Agile methodologies offers substantial benefits, enhancing the ability of organizations to respond dynamically to risks and opportunities. To demonstrate how this integration operates in practice, let's explore three detailed case studies from different industries:

Global Manufacturing Firm

Overview: A leading manufacturer of electronic components faced significant challenges related to supply chain disruptions. To address these issues, the company implemented a strategy to integrate risk management directly within its Agile project management framework.

Implementation: The firm established a real-time risk monitoring system within its Agile Project Management Office (APMO). This system utilized advanced data analytics to continuously assess risks along the supply chain, identifying potential disruptions before they could impact production.

Strategic Actions:

- **Dynamic Risk Assessments**: The firm conducted daily risk assessments using data gathered from IoT devices along the supply chain.

- **Agile Procurement Adjustments**: Based on the insights gained from ongoing risk assessments, procurement strategies were dynamically adjusted, allowing the firm to preempt potential shortages and mitigate risks associated with supplier reliability.

Outcome: The integration of ERM within an Agile framework enabled the firm to significantly reduce downtime caused by supply chain disruptions. By responding proactively to data-driven insights, the company maintained steady production rates and improved overall supply chain resilience.

Healthcare Provider During Global Health Crisis

Overview: During a significant global health crisis, a healthcare provider faced the urgent need to adapt its operations to escalating patient care demands and rapidly changing health guidelines.

Implementation: The organization adopted Agile methodologies to enhance its operational flexibility and integrated rigorous risk assessments to navigate the evolving crisis effectively.

Strategic Actions:

- **Rapid Setup of Temporary Facilities**: Agile teams quickly established temporary healthcare facilities to accommodate the increasing number of patients while adhering to safety protocols.

- **Adjustment of Care Protocols**: Leveraging continuous feedback loops, care protocols were frequently updated to reflect the latest health data and research findings, ensuring patient and staff safety.

Outcome: The agile response, underpinned by detailed risk assessments, allowed the healthcare provider to manage health risks efficiently and maintain high standards of patient care during the crisis. The organization's ability to adapt swiftly to changes was crucial in managing both operational and health-related risks effectively.

Financial Services Company

Overview: A financial services company sought to launch a new online banking platform. Recognizing the critical importance of cybersecurity, the company integrated risk management into its Agile development cycles.

Implementation: Cybersecurity risk assessments were embedded into each phase of the Agile development process, from initial design to final deployment, ensuring continuous evaluation and adaptation.

Strategic Actions:

- **Early Vulnerability Identification**: By integrating security testing into daily builds and sprints, the team identified and addressed vulnerabilities early in the development process.

- **Continuous Compliance Checks**: Compliance with financial regulations was verified continuously through automated tools and expert reviews, maintaining legal compliance and safeguarding customer data.

Outcome: The proactive approach to cybersecurity allowed the company to enhance the security of its online banking platform significantly. By identifying and mitigating risks early, the platform met all compliance requirements and launched successfully with robust security measures in place.

These case studies illustrate the practical benefits of integrating Enterprise Risk Management with Agile strategies, demonstrating how different sectors can apply these practices to manage risks proactively and maintain operational flexibility.

Integrating enterprise risk management with strategic agility is essential for organizations that wish to navigate complex, high-risk environments successfully. By adopting agile approaches to risk management, organizations can not only react swiftly to immediate challenges but also anticipate and prepare for future risks, ensuring sustainable success.

Leadership Roles in Fostering Strategic Agility

The successful implementation of strategic agility within an organization largely depends on its leadership. Leaders not only set the direction and pace of change but also create the environment that either fosters or hinders agile responsiveness. This section explores the critical roles leaders play in promoting strategic agility, detailing how they can effectively guide their organizations through agile transformations and ensure sustained agility at all levels.

Fostering an Agile Mindset

Leadership in agile environments goes beyond managing tasks and timelines; it involves fostering an agile mindset throughout the organization. This mindset is characterized by flexibility, proactive change management, and continuous improvement.

- **Modeling Agility**: Leaders must exemplify agility in their actions and decisions. This includes showing willingness to pivot strategies quickly, embracing innovative solutions, and responding promptly to feedback and changing market conditions.

- **Communicating the Value of Agility**: Leaders should continuously communicate the importance and benefits of agility to the organization. This includes articulating how agile practices can lead to better outcomes, faster responses to market opportunities, and enhanced competitiveness.

- **Encouraging Experimentation**: Promote a culture where experimentation is encouraged, and failures are seen as opportunities to learn and grow. Leaders should highlight successful adaptations and innovations that were born from risk-taking.

Strategic Decision-Making in Agile Environments

Agile strategic decision-making involves making informed decisions quickly and adapting them as more information becomes available. This dynamic approach requires leaders to balance decisiveness with flexibility.

- **Data-Driven Decisions**: Empower decision-making with real-time data and analytics. Leaders should foster an environment where decisions are made based on up-to-date, accurate information, and where data analytics tools are readily available to teams.

- **Decentralization of Decision-Making**: To enhance agility, decision-making powers should be decentralized. Leaders should trust and empower lower-level managers and team leaders to make strategic decisions, which speeds up the process and enhances responsiveness.

- **Regular Strategic Reviews**: Instead of annual strategic reviews, implement regular review cycles that allow for the timely adjustment of strategies to fit changing external conditions. These reviews should be quick, focused, and result in actionable insights.

Building and Leading Agile Teams

The construction and leadership of teams play a pivotal role in an organization's agile transformation. Agile teams are cross-functional, highly collaborative, and self-managing, and require a different style of leadership.

- **Team Composition**: Leaders should carefully compose teams to ensure a mix of skills, experiences, and perspectives. Diversity within teams can enhance problem-solving capabilities and creative thinking.

- **Empowering Team Leaders**: Equip team leaders with the tools, authority, and responsibility they need to manage their teams effectively. This involves training leaders in agile methodologies, leadership skills, and conflict resolution.

- **Continuous Feedback and Support**: Provide teams with continuous feedback and the necessary support to navigate challenges. This includes regular check-ins, access to resources, and support in overcoming obstacles.

Leaders play a crucial role in embedding and sustaining strategic agility within an organization. By fostering an agile mindset, facilitating agile decision-making, and building capable and empowered teams, leaders can ensure that their organizations are not only prepared to face the uncertainties of today but are also positioned to seize the opportunities of tomorrow. In doing so, they cultivate an enduring culture of agility that permeates every level of the organization.

Chapter 3: Organizational Design for Agility

Traditional organizational structures, designed for stability and predictability, often fail to meet the demands of today's dynamic business environment. As markets evolve and technology accelerates, organizations must embrace agility not only in their processes but also in their very design. Agile organizations are structured to adapt quickly, foster innovation, and respond effectively to external pressures.

Organizational design for agility involves more than flattening hierarchies or creating cross-functional teams. It requires a holistic approach that aligns strategy, culture, leadership, and workflows to create a responsive and resilient organization. Agile organizations empower employees at all levels, prioritize collaboration, and utilize technology to enable seamless coordination and continuous improvement.

This chapter explores how organizations can transform their structures to support agility. We will discuss the principles of agile organizational design, strategies for fostering collaboration and adaptability, and real-world examples of companies that have successfully implemented these changes. By understanding and applying these principles, leaders can create organizations that thrive in complexity and remain competitive in an ever-changing landscape.

Foundations of Agile Organizational Design

In the rapidly evolving business landscape, where disruptive technologies and shifting market dynamics are commonplace, organizational agility has emerged as a critical competency. This section explores the foundational aspects of organizational agility, exploring why it is essential and how it forms the bedrock of competitive strategy in modern enterprises.

Understanding Organizational Agility

Organizational agility refers to the ability of an organization to renew itself, adapt, change quickly, and succeed in a rapidly changing, ambiguous, turbulent environment. Agility is the capability of an organization to rapidly change or adapt in response to changes in the market. A high degree of organizational agility can help a company to react successfully to the emergence of new competitors, the development of new industry-changing technologies, or sudden shifts in overall market conditions.

Organizational agility requires a balance between stability and nimbleness, as well as the ability to navigate complexity while simplifying processes where possible. The diagram below illustrates how organizations can strategically position themselves along these dimensions to enhance resilience, collaboration, and adaptability. By adopting customized strategies and fostering interdisciplinary teamwork, organizations can respond effectively to uncertainty and change.

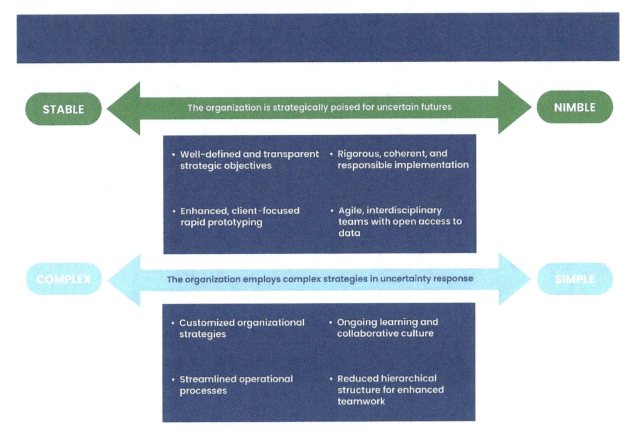

Figure: Strategies for Agile Organizations

- **Definition and Core Elements**: Agility combines elements of flexibility, balance, adaptability, and coordination under one umbrella. It is not just about the speed of response, but also about the ability to manage and lead effective change. Agile organizations are characterized by being adaptable, flexible, creative, and resilient, all traits that allow them to thrive during times of change and uncertainty.

- **Strategic Flexibility**: At its core, strategic flexibility involves the ability to respond to various demands from dynamic environments without enduring a significant penalty in time, effort, cost, or performance. This involves making organizational structures, strategies, and policies more malleable and less rigid.

Global Trends Driving the Need for Agility

Several global trends underscore the necessity for organizations to develop agility to not just survive but thrive:

- **Technological Advancements**: Rapid advancements in AI, IoT, and digital platforms are disrupting traditional business models, necessitating agile responses to integrate new technologies and capitalize on digital transformation opportunities.

- **Changing Workforce Demographics**: With more millennials and Gen Z entering the workforce, there is a growing demand for flexible work environments, a greater focus on work-life balance, and a shift toward project-based work, all of which require agile organizational practices to attract and retain top talent.

- **Consumer Behavior and Expectations**: Today's consumers expect personalization, innovation, and speed, driving companies to adapt their offerings more swiftly in response to consumer demands and market changes.

- **Globalization and Market Dynamics**: The global nature of business today requires companies to be agile enough to respond to economic, political, and social changes from different parts of the world.

Importance of Strategic Agility

Strategic agility is paramount for companies wishing to leverage opportunities and dodge threats in a timely manner. Here's why it is crucial:

- **Enhanced Competitiveness**: Agile organizations can outmaneuver larger, established competitors by innovating more quickly and responding to market changes more effectively.

- **Increased Speed to Market**: By reducing bureaucracy and enhancing collaboration, agile organizations can shorten product development cycles and bring innovations to market faster.

- **Resilience to Disruptions**: Agile organizations are better prepared to handle disruptions, whether they are economic downturns, technological shifts, or competitive threats.

- **Employee Satisfaction and Retention**: Agile environments often correlate with higher job satisfaction due to their emphasis on empowerment, accountability, and collaborative work styles.

Understanding the foundational elements of organizational agility allows leaders to begin contemplating how to structure and steer their organizations toward more fluid, responsive operational models. By embracing the principles discussed, companies can start to dismantle rigid hierarchies, encourage a culture of innovation, and ultimately, drive sustained success in an unpredictable world.

Architecting Agile Organizations

Transitioning to an agile organizational structure requires more than just an understanding of its principles; it demands a meticulous design process that aligns the structural elements of the organization with agile methodologies. This section explores the detailed strategies and approaches for designing organizations that not only embrace agility but are also optimized to thrive in dynamic and complex environments.

Structural Design for Agility

Agile organizational structures facilitate rapid decision-making and adaptability. They are fundamentally different from traditional hierarchical structures and are characterized by features that promote responsiveness and innovation.

An Agile organization is one that integrates practices, tools, and methodologies across all its functions—IT, marketing, human resources, and beyond. The diagram below illustrates a comprehensive model of an Agile organization, emphasizing iterative learning, cross-functional strategies, and progressive design thinking. By fostering collaboration across departments and adopting tailored Agile frameworks, organizations can enhance their responsiveness and innovation.

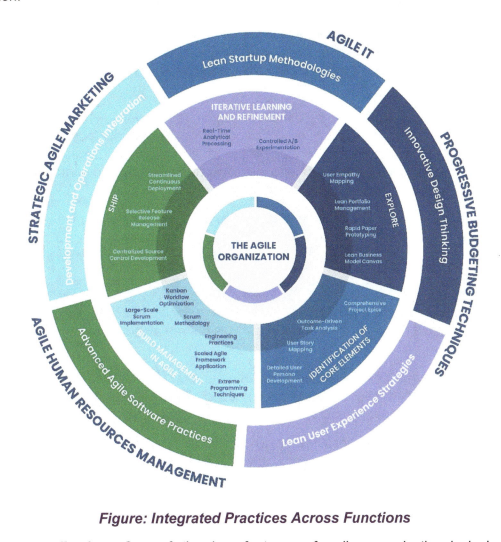

Figure: Integrated Practices Across Functions

- **Decentralization**: One of the key features of agile organizational design is the decentralization of authority. Pushing decision-making down and across the organization empowers employees and enhances the organization's ability to respond swiftly to changes and opportunities.

- **Cross-functional Teams**: Agile organizations often rely on cross-functional teams that bring together diverse skills and perspectives necessary for innovation. These teams are self-managing and are given the autonomy to plan and execute their work, which enhances speed and reduces bottlenecks in decision-making.

- **Modular Structure**: Adopting a modular structure in which the organization is composed of smaller, semi-autonomous units ('pods') that can operate independently but are coordinated in a way that they contribute to the organization's overall strategy. This setup allows for flexibility in scaling and adapting operations without disrupting the entire organization.

Agile Leadership Structures

Leadership in agile organizations does not conform to traditional top-down command and control models. Instead, it supports a more collaborative and facilitative approach.

- **Servant Leadership**: Agile organizations often thrive under servant leadership, where leaders prioritize the needs of their team and help them perform as highly as possible. Servant leaders focus on providing the resources and support needed for team members to succeed.

- **Leadership as a Role, Not a Position**: In agile organizations, leadership is often seen as a role that various members can assume, rather than a static position held by a few. This fluidity allows leadership to emerge based on context and necessity, ensuring that the most appropriate people can lead initiatives or projects based on their expertise and skills.

- **Cultivating Leaders at All Levels**: Agile organizations benefit from developing leadership skills at all levels of the organization. This approach ensures a deep bench of talent capable of stepping into leadership roles as needed, facilitating resilience and adaptability.

Innovative Team Configurations

Configuring teams in an agile organization requires a strategic approach to ensure that teams are not only well-equipped to handle their immediate tasks but are also capable of adapting to future challenges.

- **Dynamic Teaming**: Agile organizations often employ dynamic teaming practices where teams are formed and disbanded as needed. This fluid team structure allows the organization to allocate resources where they are most needed quickly.

- **Embedding Innovation into Teams**: To foster a culture of innovation, teams should be configured with a mix of roles specifically designed to focus on innovation. These might include roles such as innovation advocates or technology scouts who bring new ideas into the team.

- **Balancing Core and Adaptive Functions**: While agile teams are adaptive by nature, it's crucial to balance this with core functions that maintain the organization's ongoing operations. Hybrid teams that manage both core and adaptive functions can ensure stability while pursuing innovation.

Designing an agile organization involves a thoughtful approach to structure, leadership, and team dynamics. By decentralizing authority, empowering cross-functional teams, and fostering leadership throughout the organization, companies can create environments that are not just responsive to change but are also proactive in driving innovation. This strategic approach to organizational design is pivotal in maintaining competitiveness in rapidly evolving markets.

Cultural Transformation and Metrics

Successfully transitioning to an agile organizational design requires not only structural and procedural changes but also deep-seated shifts in corporate culture. This section examines the cultural adaptations necessary for supporting agility and introduces effective strategies for implementing and measuring these changes to ensure sustainable agile transformation.

Cultural Adaptations for Supporting Agility

Transforming an organization's culture to support agility involves reshaping long-held beliefs and practices to foster a more dynamic and responsive environment.

- **Fostering a Culture of Innovation**: Cultivating a culture that encourages creativity and continual innovation is crucial in agile environments. This involves encouraging risk-taking by providing a safe space where failure is seen as an opportunity for learning and growth. Leaders should champion innovative thinking and reward initiative and novel ideas that drive the organization forward.

- **Building Resilience**: Agile organizations must be resilient, capable of withstanding and quickly recovering from setbacks. Building resilience involves training teams to adapt to unforeseen challenges without significant performance loss. Resilience training might include scenario planning exercises and resilience workshops that help employees develop personal and team-based coping strategies.

- **Promoting Open Communication**: Transparency and open lines of communication are foundational to agile culture. Organizations should implement regular 'town hall' meetings, open forums, and digital communication platforms that facilitate a free exchange of ideas and feedback across all levels of the organization. Encouraging senior leaders to regularly share insights and strategic updates also promotes a more inclusive and communicative workplace.

Implementing and Measuring Agility

To ensure that the shift towards an agile culture is more than just nominal, organizations must implement specific metrics and KPIs to measure effectiveness and guide ongoing improvements.

- **Defining Agile Metrics**: Identify and define key performance indicators (KPIs) that accurately reflect the organization's agility goals. Common metrics might include the speed of decision-making, the rate of innovation adoption, employee engagement levels, and customer satisfaction scores. These metrics should be closely aligned with the overall strategic objectives of the organization.

- **Agile Dashboards and Reporting Tools**: Implement agile dashboards that track these KPIs in real-time, providing ongoing visibility into how well the organization is adapting to agile practices. These tools can help managers and leaders make informed decisions about where to focus resources and which areas might require more intensive cultural interventions.

- **Continuous Feedback Mechanisms**: Establish mechanisms for continuous feedback from employees at all levels. This might include regular surveys, suggestion boxes, and feedback sessions that are explicitly designed to gather insights on the agile transformation process. Utilizing this feedback can help leaders adjust strategies and processes to better meet the needs and expectations of their workforce.

- **Evaluating the Impact of Agility Initiatives**: Regularly review the impact of agility initiatives using the defined metrics and feedback. This evaluation should not only assess the immediate outcomes but also examine long-term trends to ensure that agility is being embedded deeply within the organizational culture. Adjustments and refinements should be made based on this analysis to continually enhance the effectiveness of agile practices.

The journey toward organizational agility is complex and multifaceted, involving significant cultural shifts and the careful monitoring of progress through robust metrics. By fostering a culture of innovation, resilience, and open communication, and by rigorously implementing and measuring agility initiatives, organizations can effectively navigate this transition, ensuring that agility becomes a core aspect of their operational and strategic ethos.

Case Studies and Practical Implementation

The practical implementation of agile organizational designs offers invaluable insights into the benefits, challenges, and strategies associated with transitioning to agility. This section examines real-world case studies, outlines change management strategies, and explores how continuous learning and development can sustain agility over time. Finally, it summarizes key takeaways and provides a call to action for leaders to embrace agile practices in their organizations.

Comprehensive Case Studies

Real-world examples illustrate the adaptability and success of agile organizational designs across a variety of industries. The following detailed case studies showcase how organizations from technology, healthcare, and retail have implemented agile transformations to overcome challenges, achieve innovation, and improve outcomes. Each case also highlights the obstacles faced during the transition and the strategies used to address them.

Technology Company Reimagines Team Structures

Overview: A global technology company specializing in software and hardware development faced increasing pressure from competitors who were consistently launching products faster. The company's slow product development cycles and rigid organizational structure hindered its ability to respond effectively to market demands.

Agile Transformation:

- The organization restructured its teams around **cross-functional, autonomous units**. Each team included members from development, quality assurance, and user experience, ensuring that all critical skills were present within each unit to handle tasks from start to finish.

- Teams were granted greater decision-making authority, reducing dependencies on upper management for approvals, which had previously slowed progress.

Challenges Encountered:

- **Resistance from Middle Management**: Middle managers, whose roles became less centralized, expressed concerns about their changing responsibilities. They were uncertain about their new roles within the autonomous team framework.

- **Shifting Leadership Dynamics**: Senior leaders needed to adopt a more facilitative leadership style, moving away from traditional top-down control.

Solutions and Outcomes:

- **Focused Communication and Leadership Workshops**: Leadership workshops and open forums were organized to clarify the goals and benefits of the agile model, easing concerns and building trust.

- **Measurable Improvements**: Within a year of adopting the new structure, the company reported a 30% reduction in time-to-market for new products and an increase in employee engagement scores, attributed to the empowerment and autonomy granted to teams.

Healthcare Network Enhances Patient Care

Overview: A large healthcare provider network serving a diverse population faced inefficiencies in patient care delivery. Departments operated in silos, leading to fragmented care, longer wait times, and dissatisfaction among both patients and healthcare staff.

Agile Transformation:

- The organization implemented **integrated care teams**, bringing together specialists, nurses, and administrative staff into cohesive units focused on holistic patient care.

- Agile workflows were introduced to streamline processes, enabling the network to adapt to patient needs and external regulations quickly.

Challenges Encountered:

- **Resistance to Change**: Staff accustomed to hierarchical workflows and department-specific responsibilities found it difficult to adjust to cross-functional teamwork.

- **Coordination Across Facilities**: Ensuring that agile practices were implemented consistently across multiple locations was an ongoing logistical challenge.

Solutions and Outcomes:

- **Targeted Training Programs**: The network offered training sessions tailored to each role, emphasizing the benefits of integrated care and agile workflows for improving patient outcomes.

- **Continuous Feedback Loops**: Regular feedback from staff and patients was used to fine-tune workflows and address pain points.

- **Improved Metrics**: The agile transformation resulted in a 25% reduction in patient wait times and higher patient satisfaction scores, while staff reported feeling more engaged due to better collaboration and clearer shared goals.

Retailer Innovates with Agile Hubs

Overview: A global retail chain faced stiff competition from smaller, more agile competitors who were launching innovative products and responding to market trends faster. The retailer struggled with slow innovation cycles and misaligned internal processes that delayed product development.

Agile Transformation:

- The company created **agile innovation hubs**—semi-autonomous teams tasked with exploring new product ideas and testing them rapidly. These hubs were designed to operate independently while remaining aligned with the company's broader strategic objectives.

- Each hub was staffed with a mix of marketing, product development, and customer service professionals to ensure end-to-end accountability for product launches.

Challenges Encountered:

- **Alignment with Corporate Strategy**: Ensuring that the innovation hubs did not stray too far from the company's overarching goals required careful oversight and regular communication.

- **Cultural Adjustments**: Employees needed to shift their mindset from traditional, linear workflows to the iterative, experimental processes characteristic of agile hubs.

Solutions and Outcomes:

- **Strategic Goal-Setting**: Regular alignment meetings were held between the hubs and corporate leadership to ensure their initiatives supported the company's overall strategy.

- **Cultural Reinforcement**: Workshops and success showcases highlighted the value of agility, gradually embedding it into the company's culture.

- **Results Achieved**: The innovation hubs accelerated product development cycles by 40%, allowing the retailer to respond to market trends more effectively. Additionally, customer satisfaction increased as new, more relevant products reached stores faster.

These case studies demonstrate that agile organizational design is adaptable and effective across diverse industries, including technology, healthcare, and retail. While each organization faced unique challenges, their successful transformations underscore the importance of clear communication, targeted training, and alignment with strategic objectives. By learning from these examples, other organizations can confidently embark on their own journey toward agility, reaping the benefits of faster innovation, enhanced collaboration, and improved outcomes.

Change Management Strategies

Transitioning to an agile organizational design involves significant changes, often accompanied by resistance and uncertainty. Effective change management strategies can ensure smoother transitions and sustained momentum.

- **Stakeholder Engagement**: Actively involve stakeholders at all levels—executives, managers, and team members—from the outset. Clear communication about the purpose and benefits of agility fosters buy-in and reduces resistance.

- **Managing Resistance**: Resistance to change is natural. Address concerns through open forums, one-on-one conversations, and data-driven demonstrations of how agile practices lead to improved outcomes. Celebrate small wins during the transition to build confidence and enthusiasm.

- **Maintaining Momentum During Scaling**: Scaling agility requires consistent reinforcement of agile principles. Utilize change agents or champions who can drive adoption within their teams. Provide ongoing support through training programs and agile coaching to ensure sustained alignment with agile practices as the organization grows.

Continuous Learning and Development

Continuous learning is a cornerstone of agile organizations, ensuring teams and leaders remain equipped to adapt to evolving challenges and opportunities.

- **Embedding Learning into Daily Practices**: Incorporate learning opportunities into everyday workflows, such as retrospectives, knowledge-sharing sessions, and cross-team collaborations. These activities reinforce a culture of continuous improvement.

- **Formal Training Programs**: Invest in formal training programs that focus on both technical skills and soft skills, such as collaboration, communication, and adaptability. Ensure these programs are tailored to the needs of the organization and the specific roles within it.

- **Leveraging Technology for Learning**: Utilize learning management systems (LMS) and digital platforms to provide on-demand training and resources. These tools enable employees to access learning materials at their convenience, fostering self-directed growth.

- **Measuring Learning Outcomes**: Regularly assess the effectiveness of training programs through feedback and performance metrics. Use these insights to refine learning initiatives and align them more closely with organizational goals.

Designing and maintaining agile organizations requires a holistic approach encompassing cultural transformation, structural redesign, and robust change management strategies. The case studies presented highlight the successes and challenges of adopting agility, offering lessons for other organizations on similar journeys.

Leaders are encouraged to assess their current organizational structures critically and explore opportunities for embedding agile practices. By adopting agile methodologies, fostering continuous learning, and proactively managing change, organizations can position themselves to thrive in dynamic, competitive environments.

Chapter 4: Agile Project Management Essentials

Delivering successful projects in a fast-paced, ever-evolving environment requires a fresh approach to project management. Agile project management has emerged as a vital methodology, offering the flexibility, collaboration, and iterative processes necessary to address complex challenges and deliver value consistently. It empowers teams to respond quickly to changes, prioritize effectively, and maintain a laser focus on customer needs.

Unlike traditional project management, which often follows rigid timelines and predefined plans, Agile project management embraces adaptability and continuous feedback. It shifts the focus from simply completing tasks to achieving outcomes that align with business objectives and user expectations. This mindset fosters innovation, minimizes waste, and ensures that projects remain on track even in the face of uncertainty.

In this chapter, we explore the key principles and practices of Agile project management. From understanding the fundamentals of iterative planning and incremental delivery to leveraging tools and frameworks that enhance collaboration and efficiency, this chapter provides actionable insights for managing Agile projects successfully. Whether leading a small team or coordinating across multiple departments, mastering these essentials is critical for any leader navigating the complexities of modern project management.

Agile Project Management Frameworks

Overview of Agile Frameworks

Agile project management is characterized by its flexibility, iterative development, and focus on customer collaboration and responsiveness to change. Various Agile frameworks offer different structures and practices suited to various types of projects and organizational environments. Key frameworks include:

- **Scrum**: Scrum is one of the most popular Agile frameworks, particularly suited to projects with rapidly changing or highly emergent requirements. It organizes work in fixed-length iterations called sprints, typically lasting two to four weeks, with daily meetings (daily scrums) to discuss progress and roadblocks.

  The Scrum framework is one of the most widely adopted methodologies within Agile project management. It provides a structured approach to iterative delivery, focusing on clear roles, well-defined processes, and continuous feedback. The diagram below illustrates how Scrum works, from stakeholder input and sprint planning to execution, reviews, and retrospectives. Each component of this workflow ensures that teams remain aligned with project objectives while adapting to changes efficiently.

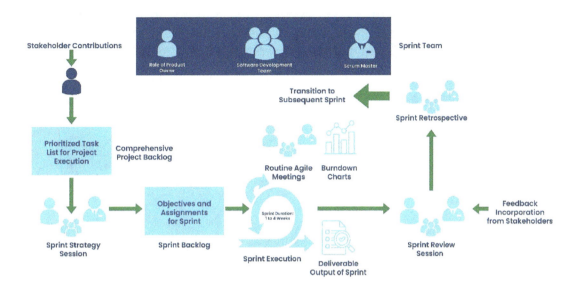

How Scrum Framework Works

Figure: Scrum Framework

- **Kanban**: Unlike Scrum, Kanban is a continuous flow method that focuses on visualizing work processes and limiting work-in-progress (WIP) to improve flow and reduce bottlenecks. It is ideal for teams that require flexibility in task prioritization and completion.

- **Lean**: Lean software development is derived from lean manufacturing practices and principles. It emphasizes optimizing efficiency, minimizing waste, and delivering value to the customer quickly and efficiently.

Selecting the Right Framework

Choosing the right Agile framework depends on various factors, including the project's complexity, team size, and specific business objectives. Here's how to make an informed choice:

- **Project Complexity and Size**: Scrum is well-suited for complex projects where requirements change frequently, while Kanban is preferable for projects that have varying priorities and less defined schedules. Lean is ideal when efficiency and waste reduction are priorities.

- **Team Dynamics and Workflow**: Consider how your team works best. Scrum requires disciplined adherence to sprint schedules and roles, making it suitable for teams that thrive under structured conditions. Kanban offers more flexibility and is ideal for teams that manage ongoing maintenance or continuous delivery.

- **Organizational Goals**: Align the framework with strategic business objectives. For example, if rapid innovation is a key goal, Scrum's sprint reviews and retrospectives provide regular opportunities for reassessment and iteration, which can drive faster innovation.

Integrating Frameworks into Existing Processes

Integrating an Agile framework into existing project management processes can be challenging but rewarding. Consider these strategies:

- **Gradual Implementation**: Start small by implementing Agile practices in smaller teams or projects before rolling them out organization-wide. This allows the organization to adapt to Agile methodologies without overwhelming existing structures.

- **Training and Support**: Provide comprehensive training and ongoing support to all stakeholders involved in the process. Understanding the Agile principles and practices is crucial for effective implementation.

- **Hybrid Approaches**: In some cases, a hybrid approach that combines traditional project management methods with Agile practices can be effective. This approach allows teams to gradually adapt to Agile while still maintaining some familiarity with their previous processes.

Understanding the different Agile frameworks and how they can be effectively implemented in an organization is crucial for executives looking to enhance their project management strategies. Each framework offers unique benefits, and the choice depends on the specific needs and conditions of the project and team.

Let's expand on each aspect of Tools and Technologies for Agile Management, adding more detail and depth to fully cover how tools and technology facilitate effective Agile project management, especially in the domains of software engineering and architecture.

Tools and Technologies for Agile Management

Essential Tools for Agile Project Management

In Agile project management, the right tools can make a significant difference in team productivity and project success. These tools help in organizing tasks, managing project timelines, and enhancing team communication, which are critical for Agile environments.

- **Digital Kanban Boards**: Tools like Trello and Asana provide visual workflows that are integral for teams practicing Kanban. They allow teams to create tasks, assign them, and move them through different stages of the development process visually. Jira offers more robust functionalities tailored for Agile, including sprint planning features, custom workflows, and detailed reporting capabilities, making it suitable for more complex projects.

- **Project Tracking Software**: For Scrum teams, software like Jira Agile and VersionOne offers specialized features such as sprint planning tools, user story mapping, and release planning. These platforms are designed to accommodate the iterative nature of Agile by allowing teams to plan, execute, and review their sprints in a centralized location.

- **Collaboration Platforms**: Slack and Microsoft Teams are critical for maintaining daily communication, integrating with other tools, and facilitating quick discussions and decision-making. These platforms support channels for specific topics, direct messaging, and integration with other Agile tools, creating a dynamic environment where information flows freely across the team.

Leveraging Automation in Agile Projects

Automation in Agile projects is not about replacing human input but enhancing the team's ability to deliver high-quality products efficiently.

- **Continuous Integration and Continuous Delivery (CI/CD)**: Tools like Jenkins, GitLab CI, and CircleCI automate the build and deployment processes, enabling frequent releases and ensuring that the product can be reliably released at any time. This automation supports Agile's principle of rapid and flexible response to change.

- **Automated Testing**: Automated testing tools such as Selenium for web applications, JUnit for Java applications, and QTest for managing test cases play a crucial role in Agile. They provide immediate feedback on the quality and functionality of the software, allowing teams to address issues promptly. This continuous testing is essential in a setting where changes are frequent and need to be validated quickly.

- **Performance Dashboards**: Real-time dashboards provide a snapshot of key project metrics at a glance. Tools like Grafana and Tableau can be connected to various data sources to track everything from sprint progress and release readiness to more granular metrics like code commits and bug resolution times. These dashboards are invaluable for keeping all stakeholders informed and ensuring decisions are data-driven.

Virtual Collaboration in Agile Teams

The rise of distributed teams has made virtual collaboration tools indispensable in maintaining the cohesive operation of Agile teams.

- **Video Conferencing Tools**: Regular video conferencing is crucial for maintaining personal connections and ensuring clear communication. Tools like Zoom and Google Meet help simulate a face-to-face interaction environment, crucial for effective daily stand-ups, sprint reviews, and retrospectives.

- **Real-Time Document Editing**: Collaborative document tools such as Google Docs and Microsoft Office Online allow team members to work on user stories, sprint plans, and technical documentation in real time, ensuring that all team members have the most current information at all times.

- **Secure Instant Messaging Platforms**: Beyond facilitating quick communication, platforms like Slack and Microsoft Teams can be configured to meet higher security standards necessary for projects in sensitive industries, ensuring that project communications are both efficient and secure.

The selection and effective utilization of appropriate tools and technologies are fundamental to the success of Agile project management. These tools enhance the Agile capabilities of teams by supporting the principles of transparency, efficiency, and continuous improvement, crucial for the dynamic field of software engineering and architecture.

Let's expand further on each component of Executing Agile Projects, adding depth and detail to thoroughly cover how Agile projects are executed effectively, particularly in environments like software engineering and architecture.

Executing Agile Projects

Planning and Executing Sprints

Sprint planning and execution form the backbone of Agile project management. This structured approach allows teams to address complex tasks by breaking them down into more manageable, time-boxed periods known as sprints.

- **Sprint Planning**: This crucial session involves the entire team and focuses on defining what can be delivered in the upcoming sprint and how the work will be achieved. It begins with the product owner presenting the prioritized backlog items to be considered for the sprint, followed by the team discussing, estimating, and committing to the tasks they believe can be accomplished.

- **Daily Stand-Ups**: These short, time-boxed meetings are essential for the team to synchronize activities and plan for the next 24 hours. Each team member discusses what they've completed, plans to work on next, and any impediments they're facing. The scrum master facilitates these meetings to ensure they are focused and efficient.

- **Sprint Reviews and Retrospectives**: The sprint ends with these two critical meetings. The review involves stakeholders and is an opportunity to showcase the work done, gathering feedback that may adjust the product backlog. The retrospective is internal to the team and focuses on process improvement—what went well, what didn't, and how processes could be optimized moving forward.

Managing Agile Project Risks

Risk management is proactive and continuous in Agile projects, ensuring that potential issues are addressed before they become problematic.

- **Proactive Risk Identification**: During sprint planning and daily stand-ups, teams should actively discuss potential risks. This continuous vigilance helps in early detection and mitigation.

- **Risk Prioritization and Response Planning**: Identified risks are evaluated and prioritized based on their potential impact and probability. Responses are planned according to their priority, focusing on mitigating high-impact risks through strategic adjustments in project scope, resources, or timelines.

- **Executive Oversight and Support**: Executives play a key role by providing support for risk mitigation strategies and ensuring that there are adequate resources available to address significant risks. They should also foster a culture where discussing risks openly is encouraged and supported.

Agile Budgeting and Resource Allocation

Agile budgeting and resource allocation are dynamic, evolving with the project's needs and the insights gained from each sprint.

- **Iterative Budgeting**: Budget reviews are integrated into sprint reviews, allowing adjustments based on project progress and feedback. This flexibility supports the Agile commitment to adapting to change and delivering the highest value.

- **Flexible Resource Allocation**: Agile projects may require fluid resource allocation, with team members shifting roles or tasks as needed. This approach maximizes the utilization of skills and expertise within the team, adapting to the project's evolving requirements.

- **Continuous Monitoring and Adjustment**: Utilizing tools like Jira or Microsoft Project, executives can monitor budget and resource usage in real-time, making adjustments to ensure the project remains on track financially and operationally. This ongoing monitoring is crucial to maintaining the agility needed to respond to new information or project shifts.

Executing Agile projects demands a structured yet flexible approach to planning, risk management, and budgeting. These elements are crucial for maintaining the momentum of Agile projects and ensuring their success, providing continuous delivery of value to stakeholders and alignment with strategic business goals.

Enhancing Team Performance in Agile Projects

Fostering High-Performance Agile Teams

Creating and sustaining high-performance teams is pivotal in Agile environments, where the pace and scope of work can change rapidly. Here's how executives and team leaders can foster such teams:

- **Clear Goals and Alignment**: Ensure that every team member understands the project goals and how their work contributes to these objectives. Alignment with the broader vision motivates team members by showing the impact of their contributions.

- **Empowerment and Autonomy**: Empower teams by delegating decision-making authority. This empowerment increases job satisfaction and ownership, driving team members to perform at their best. Facilitate an environment where team members feel confident in taking initiative without constant oversight.

- **Continuous Skill Development**: Agile teams need to adapt and learn rapidly to keep pace with evolving project demands. Support this by providing ongoing education and training opportunities, such as workshops, courses, and access to learning resources. Encourage a culture of knowledge sharing within the team, where more experienced members mentor others.

1Leadership Roles in Agile Projects

Leadership in Agile teams differs significantly from traditional project management. Here are key roles and responsibilities:

- **Servant Leadership**: The concept of servant leadership is integral in Agile. Leaders serve their teams by removing impediments, facilitating processes, and supporting personal and professional growth. This style enhances team cohesion and productivity.

- **Coaching and Mentoring**: Agile leaders act as coaches and mentors rather than commanders. They guide teams through the Agile process, help resolve interpersonal issues, and ensure the team maintains its focus on Agile principles.

- **Performance Feedback**: Provide regular and constructive feedback. Agile leaders should conduct performance reviews in a manner that is consistent with Agile values—collaborative and forward-looking, focusing on continuous improvement rather than punitive measures.

1 Scaling Agile Practices Across the Organization

As Agile practices prove successful within teams, scaling them across the organization can multiply their benefits. Here's how to effectively scale Agile practices:

- **Consistent Frameworks and Processes**: When scaling Agile, maintaining consistency in frameworks and processes helps ensure that teams across the organization can collaborate effectively. Use common tools and methodologies to keep everyone on the same page.

- **Inter-Team Coordination**: Establish structures and meetings that facilitate communication and coordination between teams. Practices like Scrum of Scrums, where representatives from each team meet to discuss progress and challenges, can be effective.

- **Cultural Consistency**: Ensure that Agile values—like collaboration, responsiveness to change, and customer focus—are embedded in the organization's culture. This cultural alignment is crucial as more teams adopt Agile methods, helping to prevent silos and ensuring that Agile scales successfully.

Enhancing team performance in Agile projects requires a combination of clear goal setting, empowering leadership, continuous learning, and effective scaling strategies. By focusing on these areas, executives can ensure that their teams not only adopt Agile practices but excel at them, delivering superior results and driving organizational success in competitive environments.

Chapter 5: Cultivating an Agile Culture

Agile methodologies are not just about processes and tools—they are fundamentally about people and culture. For organizations to truly embrace agility, they must foster a culture that values collaboration, adaptability, innovation, and continuous learning. This cultural transformation is often the most challenging yet rewarding aspect of adopting Agile practices.

An Agile culture is one where individuals feel empowered to take initiative, where teams are aligned around shared goals, and where feedback and experimentation drive improvement. It prioritizes trust, open communication, and a commitment to delivering value to customers. Cultivating such a culture requires intentional effort from leaders at all levels, who must embody Agile principles in their actions and decisions.

In this chapter, we explore the strategies for building and sustaining an Agile culture. From aligning organizational values with Agile principles to implementing practices that encourage collaboration and resilience, this chapter provides a roadmap for fostering an environment where agility can thrive. By focusing on people and culture, leaders can unlock the full potential of Agile, driving innovation and adaptability in their organizations.

Understanding Agile Culture

Defining Agile Culture

An Agile culture emphasizes a set of behaviors and values that promote the Agile methodology's foundational principles—such as iterative learning, flexibility, collaboration, and customer-centricity. This culture is characterized by several key attributes:

- **Empowerment and Responsibility**: Employees at all levels are given the authority to make decisions affecting their work, encouraging a sense of ownership and accountability.

- **Open Communication**: Communication within an Agile culture is bidirectional and transparent. Information flows freely across all levels, ensuring that every team member can contribute to decision-making and innovation.

- **Respect for Individuals**: This culture values the diversity of thoughts and backgrounds, recognizing that every individual brings unique ideas and perspectives that can drive the organization forward.

- **Focus on Delivering Value**: Every action and decision is evaluated based on the value it adds to the customer, aligning the organization's output closely with customer needs and expectations.

The Importance of Culture in Agile Transformation

Cultural alignment is essential for the successful adoption of Agile methodologies. The shift to Agile involves more than just changing processes and tools; it requires a transformation in the way people think and work.

- **Driving Behavioral Change**: An Agile culture promotes behaviors that are necessary for Agile methods to be effective, such as flexibility in response to changing requirements and a proactive attitude towards problem-solving.

- **Sustaining Change**: Culture is the backbone that supports and sustains changes in organizational processes. A strong Agile culture ensures that Agile practices are not just implemented but are embedded and enduring, resisting the drift back to old ways of working.

- **Enhancing Collaboration and Innovation**: Agile culture fosters an environment where teamwork and creativity are at the forefront. It breaks down barriers between departments and encourages cross-functional collaboration, which is vital for innovation and rapid problem-solving.

- **Improving Organizational Resilience**: Organizations with a robust Agile culture are better equipped to handle market volatility and adapt to new challenges quickly. This resilience becomes a competitive advantage, enabling the organization to navigate complexities more effectively than its competitors.

Understanding these cultural elements and their impact on an organization's transition to Agile is critical for leaders. By fostering an Agile culture, executives ensure that the transition is not only successful in the short term but also sustainable in the long term, leading to continuous improvement and competitive advantage.

Building the Foundations of an Agile Culture

Leadership and Agile Culture

Leadership plays a pivotal role in shaping and nurturing an Agile culture. Effective Agile leaders foster an environment that encourages the Agile mindset and practices, enabling the organization to thrive in dynamic and competitive landscapes.

- **Modeling Agile Values**: Leaders must exemplify the core Agile values of collaboration, openness, respect, and courage. By modeling these behaviors, leaders set a standard and create a benchmark for others in the organization.

- **Supporting Team Autonomy**: Agile leaders empower teams by delegating authority and encouraging decision-making at the team level. This empowerment boosts morale and accelerates innovation, as team members feel more invested in the outcomes of their work.

- **Facilitating Continuous Learning**: Leaders should champion continuous professional development and learning. By promoting training sessions, workshops, and opportunities for skill advancement, leaders ensure that their teams remain at the cutting edge of industry standards and practices.

Establishing Core Values and Principles

Defining and embedding core Agile values and principles is crucial for building a foundation for Agile culture. These values guide the behavior and decisions of all team members and should be clearly communicated and integrated into daily activities.

- **Explicit Communication of Values**: Regularly communicate the organization's commitment to Agile values through multiple channels—meetings, newsletters, and internal communications platforms. Ensure that every new and existing employee understands what these values mean in practice.

- **Integration into Performance Metrics**: Incorporate Agile values into performance evaluations. Recognize and reward behaviors that align with these values to reinforce their importance.

- **Values in Recruitment**: Embed Agile values into the recruitment process. Assess new hires not only for technical skills but also for their fit with the organization's Agile culture, ensuring that incoming team members will support and enhance the existing culture.

Encouraging Team Collaboration and Empowerment

Collaboration and empowerment are key facets of an Agile culture. Cultivating these aspects can lead to more effective and responsive teams.

- **Cross-functional Teams**: Organize teams so that they include members from different disciplines, which encourages a diversity of perspectives and enhances problem-solving capabilities.

- **Creating Collaborative Spaces**: Design workspaces—physical or virtual—that encourage spontaneous discussions and easy sharing of ideas. Tools like digital whiteboards and collaborative software can facilitate this interaction in remote or hybrid settings.

- **Empowerment through Trust**: Trust teams to manage their workflows and make decisions related to their work. This trust fosters a sense of responsibility and accountability, essential for Agile environments.

Creating a Learning Organization

To maintain an Agile culture, organizations must continually learn and adapt. Establishing mechanisms for learning and adaptation is critical.

- **Continuous Feedback Loops**: Implement systems for regular feedback, both from within the team and from stakeholders, including customers. Use this feedback to make informed adjustments to products, processes, and strategies.

- **Learning from Failures**: Promote a culture that does not punish failure but rather views it as an opportunity for learning and growth. Encourage teams to share lessons learned from failures in a constructive way.

- **Investment in Learning Resources**: Allocate resources for ongoing education—subscriptions to industry publications, access to courses, and attendance at relevant conferences.

Building the foundations of an Agile culture requires deliberate actions and commitments from all levels of leadership. By focusing on these fundamental areas, organizations can create an environment where Agile principles flourish, leading to sustained growth and innovation.

Implementing Agile Culture Practices

Encouraging Team Collaboration and Empowerment

Creating an environment that fosters collaboration and empowers team members is crucial for Agile success. Here are specific strategies to enhance these aspects:

- **Structural Enablement for Collaboration**: Design organizational structures that facilitate cross-functional interaction. This might involve restructuring physical office layouts to promote open communication, or using virtual tools that enhance collaboration across distributed teams.

- **Empowerment through Trust and Transparency**: Trust is fundamental. Encourage managers and leaders to demonstrate trust by delegating meaningful responsibilities to team members, along with the corresponding authority to make decisions. Transparency about company goals, challenges, and successes makes this delegation more effective, as team members understand the context of their work.

- **Recognition and Reward Systems**: Implement recognition systems that reward collaborative behaviors and team achievements rather than only individual accomplishments. This can include peer recognition programs, team performance bonuses, and public acknowledgment of collaborative successes.

Creating a Learning Organization

Building a learning organization is about more than just providing training opportunities; it involves creating a culture that values ongoing development and the acquisition of knowledge.

- **Formal and Informal Learning Opportunities**: Beyond formal training sessions, promote informal learning through mentoring, coaching, and shadowing programs. Encourage employees to engage in self-directed learning by providing access to learning resources and time to explore them.

- **Creating Psychological Safety**: Establish a work environment where team members feel safe to express themselves without fear of being judged or punished. This safety is crucial for encouraging experimentation and learning from mistakes, which are integral to Agile processes.

- **Feedback Loops and Reflective Practices**: Integrate regular feedback loops into team routines, using tools like retrospectives to reflect on both what went well and what didn't. These practices should be structured to foster constructive dialogue and actionable insights.

Measuring and Adjusting Cultural Practices

To ensure that the Agile culture is effective and continues to evolve with the organization's needs, it's important to continuously measure its health and make necessary adjustments.

- **Culture Surveys and Employee Feedback**: Regularly distribute surveys and collect employee feedback to gauge the health of the Agile culture. Questions should focus on employees' perceptions of agility, empowerment, collaboration, and leadership support.

- **Data-Driven Adjustments**: Use the data from surveys and feedback mechanisms to identify trends and areas for improvement. This might involve adjusting team structures, changing communication practices, or offering additional training in specific areas.

- **Iterative Improvement**: Treat cultural adjustments as you would any Agile process—subject to iterations and improvements. Implement changes on a small scale to test their effectiveness before rolling them out organization-wide.

Implementing and sustaining an Agile culture is an ongoing journey that requires continuous effort and adaptation. By actively fostering collaboration, creating learning opportunities, and continuously measuring and refining cultural practices, organizations can build a resilient and effective Agile culture that drives innovation and project success.

Sustaining and Evolving an Agile Culture

Sustaining Agile Values Over Time

Maintaining an Agile culture as the organization grows and evolves requires continuous effort and strategic oversight. Here's how to ensure that Agile values are sustained over the long term:

- **Reinforcement of Agile Principles**: Regularly reinforce the core principles of Agile through all levels of the organization. This can involve ongoing training sessions, featured stories in company communications that highlight successful Agile projects, and leadership discussions that reiterate the value of Agile practices.

- **Leadership Commitment**: Continuous leadership commitment is crucial for sustaining an Agile culture. Leaders should consistently demonstrate Agile behaviors and decisions that reinforce the culture, serving as role models for the organization.

- **Agile Coaching**: Employ Agile coaches to help teams and individuals continuously improve their understanding and implementation of Agile practices. Coaches can also help address any deviations or misunderstandings that might arise as the organization evolves.

Addressing Cultural Challenges

As organizations implement and scale Agile practices, several cultural challenges may arise. Addressing these effectively is key to maintaining the health and effectiveness of Agile practices:

- **Resistance to Change**: Some team members or units within the organization may resist adopting Agile practices. Address this by identifying the root causes of resistance and engaging directly with the skeptics. Providing additional training, aligning Agile benefits with personal or team goals, and demonstrating the success of Agile through pilot projects can help mitigate resistance.

- **Maintaining Quality During Scaling**: As Agile practices are scaled, there can be a dilution of quality or misinterpretation of Agile principles. To combat this, standardize training and ensure consistent practices across teams. Regular audits or reviews of Agile practices can help maintain high standards and correct deviations.

- **Agile in Distributed Teams**: Agile practices can be challenging to implement in geographically distributed teams due to differences in time zones, cultures, and communication styles. Use technology effectively to bridge communication gaps, and establish clear norms that respect diverse working conditions and practices.

Future-Proofing Agile Culture

Looking ahead, it's important to future-proof the Agile culture by staying adaptable and responsive to new challenges and opportunities:

- **Incorporate New Agile Trends and Technologies**: Stay updated with the latest developments in Agile methodologies and tools. Integrating new and relevant practices can help revitalize Agile implementation and keep the organization at the cutting edge.

- **Feedback Mechanisms**: Maintain robust feedback mechanisms that allow for continuous learning from experiences. These mechanisms should evolve to capture relevant insights as the organization grows and the external environment changes.

- **Culture of Innovation**: Foster a culture that encourages experimentation and innovation not just in product development but also in process improvement and organizational practices. This helps in maintaining agility and responsiveness to market or technological changes.

Sustaining an Agile culture requires vigilance, adaptability, and a commitment to continuous improvement. By addressing challenges, reinforcing Agile values, and preparing for future developments, leaders can ensure that their organizations remain agile and responsive in a changing world.

Chapter 6: Technology and Architecture Planning

In Agile environments, technology and architecture planning must be as adaptive and iterative as the development processes they support. Traditional approaches to architectural design, which often rely on rigid upfront planning, struggle to keep pace with the rapid changes and evolving requirements of Agile projects. Instead, Agile architecture prioritizes flexibility, scalability, and continuous improvement, enabling teams to respond effectively to emerging challenges and opportunities.

Technology and architecture planning in Agile is not about sacrificing long-term vision for short-term gains—it is about balancing strategic foresight with the ability to adapt. This requires a collaborative approach where architects, developers, and stakeholders work together to ensure that architectural decisions align with business goals and user needs. The result is an architecture that evolves alongside the product, supporting innovation and reducing technical debt.

This chapter explores Agile approaches to technology and architecture planning, including best practices for iterative design, strategies for managing technical complexity, and techniques for fostering collaboration between technical and non-technical stakeholders. By mastering these principles, leaders can ensure that their teams are equipped to deliver high-quality solutions that are both robust and adaptable.

Agile Planning in Technology and Architecture

Principles of Agile Planning

In the context of technology and architectural projects, Agile planning operates under several key principles designed to enhance flexibility and ensure the delivery of maximum value:

- **Iterative Development**: This core Agile principle involves breaking projects into smaller, manageable increments or sprints, allowing for continual assessment and adaptation. It's especially beneficial in technology projects where early prototypes can be tested and refined based on user feedback.

- **Value-Driven Prioritization**: Agile planning requires a focus on delivering the highest business value in the shortest time. This involves continuous prioritization and reprioritization of project tasks based on evolving project dynamics and stakeholder inputs, ensuring that resources are always allocated to the most critical activities.

- **Responsiveness to Change**: Unlike traditional planning methods that often resist deviations from a set plan, Agile planning embraces change, allowing projects to adapt swiftly to new information or external market shifts. This flexibility is crucial in fast-paced industries like technology and architecture, where staying aligned with current trends and customer demands is essential.

Adapting Agile to Technology Strategies

Agile methodologies can be particularly effective in aligning technology projects with strategic business goals, ensuring that technological developments are not just innovative but also commercially viable and strategically relevant.

- **Strategic Integration**: Agile planning should be seamlessly integrated with the organization's strategic objectives. This ensures that every sprint delivers not just project milestones but also contributes to long-term strategic goals, such as market expansion, customer satisfaction, or technological innovation.

- **Agile Roadmapping**: Agile roadmaps provide a flexible yet clear outline of the direction of a project but allow for changes as required by stakeholder feedback or unforeseen challenges. These roadmaps are crucial in technology projects for accommodating rapid technological advancements and market changes without losing sight of the overall project goals.

- **Stakeholder Engagement**: Regular and structured engagement with stakeholders is integral to Agile planning. This includes not just the end-users but also cross-functional leaders within the organization who depend on the technology being developed. Engaging these stakeholders ensures that the project remains aligned with business needs and leverages diverse insights to enhance project outcomes.

Bridging Agile Planning with Execution

To effectively implement Agile planning in technology and architecture, bridging the gap between planning and execution is crucial. This involves practical steps to ensure that plans are actionable and directly tied to project execution:

- **Dynamic Task Management**: Utilize tools like JIRA or Asana to manage tasks dynamically. These tools help in visualizing work progress, adjusting priorities in real time, and maintaining transparency across the team.

- **Regular Sync-Ups**: Beyond the daily stand-ups, regular strategic sync-ups between project managers and business leaders can ensure that Agile projects are not just progressing according to plan but also aligned with evolving business strategies.

- **Feedback Loops**: Establish robust feedback loops that collect inputs from both users and stakeholders throughout the project lifecycle. These loops should inform every stage of the project, ensuring that the product evolves in a manner that is consistently aligned with user needs and business objectives.

Implementing Agile planning in technology and architecture requires a deep understanding of Agile principles and a commitment to integrating these principles into every aspect of project planning and execution. By fostering an environment that values flexibility, continuous improvement, and stakeholder engagement, technology leaders can ensure that their projects are successful and strategically aligned.

Tools and Techniques for Agile Technology Planning

Agile Tools for Technology Planning

To effectively implement Agile methodologies in technology and architecture planning, leveraging the right tools is crucial. These tools facilitate the management of projects in a dynamic and iterative environment, ensuring that teams can respond swiftly to changes without losing sight of the overall project goals.

- **Project Management Software**: Tools like Jira, Trello, and Asana are indispensable in Agile environments. They offer features like task boards, sprint planning capabilities, and real-time collaboration, all of which support the Agile workflows necessary for technology projects.

- **Roadmapping Tools**: Agile roadmapping tools such as Aha! and ProductPlan allow for the flexible planning of project milestones and deliverables. These tools make it easy to adjust plans based on changing priorities and provide a visual roadmap that aligns the team on the project's strategic direction.

- **Backlog Management Systems**: Effective backlog management is key in Agile planning. Tools like VersionOne and Rally help prioritize and manage the backlog, ensuring that the team is always working on the most critical tasks that provide the highest value.

Techniques for Effective Agile Architecture

Incorporating Agile methodologies into architecture planning requires techniques that support flexibility and continuous iteration without compromising the architectural integrity or scalability of the system.

- **Architectural Spikes**: Use architectural spikes to explore potential solutions to complex problems in a controlled, time-boxed manner. This technique allows architects to assess different approaches and determine the most effective path forward without committing to a full-scale development.

- **Refactoring**: Regular refactoring is essential to maintain the adaptability of the system architecture. As new features are added and the system evolves, refactoring helps ensure that the architecture remains clean, efficient, and aligned with the project's requirements.

- **Continuous Integration and Continuous Deployment (CI/CD)**: Implementing CI/CD practices in the development process ensures that changes are integrated and tested frequently, reducing integration issues and allowing for quicker adjustments to the architecture as needed.

Balancing Flexibility and Stability in Architecture

While Agile promotes flexibility and responsiveness, maintaining a stable architecture that supports long-term growth is also crucial.

- **Modular Architecture**: Design systems with modular architecture to allow parts of the system to be updated or changed independently without affecting the whole. This approach supports Agile principles by enabling quick iterations and updates.

- **Documentation and Communication**: While Agile emphasizes working software over comprehensive documentation, maintaining essential documentation for architecture is crucial. Ensure that changes and updates are well-documented and communicated to all relevant team members to prevent knowledge silos and ensure continuity.

- **Governance and Standards**: Establish clear governance practices and standards to guide architectural decisions and maintain system integrity as changes are made. This framework helps balance the need for rapid iteration with the requirement to meet regulatory and operational standards.

Utilizing effective tools and techniques is fundamental in adapting Agile methodologies to technology and architecture planning. By choosing the right project management software, employing Agile architectural techniques, and balancing flexibility with stability, organizations can ensure that their technology strategies are both innovative and sustainable.

Implementing Agile in Large-Scale Technology Projects

Implementing Agile methodologies in large-scale technology and architecture projects presents unique challenges. However, with strategic planning and effective frameworks, these challenges can be managed to deliver successful project outcomes.

Scaling Agile for Large Projects

Scaling Agile practices for larger projects involves adapting Agile methodologies to work across multiple teams and possibly across different departments or geographic locations. Here's how to effectively scale Agile in large projects:

- **Choose the Right Scaling Framework**: Frameworks like SAFe (Scaled Agile Framework), LeSS (Large-Scale Scrum), and DaD (Disciplined Agile Delivery) provide structured approaches for applying Agile at scale. These frameworks offer processes and tools designed to address the complexities of large projects, including coordination between teams, alignment with organizational goals, and management of dependencies.

- **Implement Release Trains**: In frameworks like SAFe, release trains synchronize the efforts of all teams, aligning them on a common delivery schedule. This helps ensure that multiple teams working on different parts of a project remain aligned and integrated, contributing to a cohesive final product.

- **Cross-Functional Coordination**: Establish cross-functional teams or integration teams that work across the traditional boundaries of business, technology, and operations. These teams focus on removing impediments and ensuring that the work flows smoothly across all parts of the organization involved in the project.

Case Studies: Agile in Complex Projects

Real-world examples provide valuable insights into how Agile can be effectively implemented in large and complex projects. Here are brief overviews of case studies that illustrate successful Agile implementations:

- **Global Tech Company**: A multinational corporation successfully implemented SAFe to manage a large-scale digital transformation project involving over 1,000 team members across multiple continents. By organizing around Agile Release Trains and adopting a Lean-Agile Center of Excellence, the company improved project delivery times by 30% and increased team engagement and productivity.

- **Architectural Firm**: An architectural firm adopted the LeSS framework to coordinate multiple design projects simultaneously. By structuring the organization into several smaller, cross-functional teams and focusing on continuous integration of design elements, the firm was able to respond more quickly to client feedback and reduce the overall project cycle time.

Common Challenges and Solutions

Scaling Agile in large projects often comes with several challenges:

- **Ensuring Consistency Across Teams**: With multiple teams, maintaining a consistent understanding and implementation of Agile practices can be difficult.

  - *Solution*: Regular training sessions, shared documentation, and consistent use of tools across all teams can help maintain consistency.

- **Managing Interdependencies**: Large projects often involve complex dependencies between tasks handled by different teams.

  - *Solution*: Use of dependency tracking tools and regular synchronization meetings can help manage these interdependencies effectively.

- **Preserving Agile Principles**: As projects scale, there's a risk of reverting to waterfall or other traditional project management approaches under pressure.

  - *Solution*: Strong leadership commitment to Agile principles and continuous reinforcement through coaching and mentorship are essential to preserve the Agile culture.

Successfully implementing Agile in large-scale technology projects requires careful consideration of scaling frameworks, effective coordination across teams, and strategies to overcome common challenges. By adhering to Agile principles and adapting strategies as needed, organizations can achieve scalability while maintaining the flexibility and responsiveness that Agile offers.

Let's expand on Part 4 of Chapter 6, "Maintaining Flexibility and Innovation in Agile Projects," by diving deeper into strategies that ensure agile projects remain adaptable while continuing to drive forward-looking innovation within the framework of strategic consistency.

Maintaining Flexibility and Innovation in Agile Projects

Ensuring Flexibility in Architectural Design

Flexibility in architectural design is crucial for accommodating changes without extensive overhauls. Here are advanced strategies for maintaining this flexibility:

- **Adaptive Architectural Practices**: Implement practices like evolutionary architecture, which anticipates changes and evolution as a normal part of the architectural lifecycle. Techniques such as making extensive use of APIs and service-oriented architecture can allow components to evolve independently of one another.

- **Component-Based Development**: Utilize component-based development to create systems with interchangeable parts that can be updated or replaced without impacting the entire system. This approach reduces the complexity involved in updating systems and allows easier adaptation to new technologies or business requirements.

- **Regular Architectural Assessments**: Conduct regular assessments of the architecture to ensure it continues to meet the needs of the business. These assessments can identify areas where the architecture may need to evolve to support new directions or technologies.

Promoting Innovation in Agile Teams

Innovation is vital for keeping Agile teams ahead of the curve. To foster a culture of innovation, consider these extended strategies:

- **Dedicated Innovation Roles**: Establish roles or teams specifically tasked with driving innovation within the organization. These roles can focus on emerging technologies, process improvements, and other innovations that may not fall within the normal scope of project teams.

- **Incorporating Design Thinking**: Embed design thinking processes into the project lifecycle to encourage creative problem-solving. Design thinking workshops can help teams ideate new solutions to user needs that may not be obvious through traditional analysis.

- **Leveraging Technology Incubators**: Create or partner with technology incubators that allow team members to work on side projects or new technologies that could potentially benefit the main project or the company at large. This exposure to cutting-edge developments can spur innovation within the team.

Balancing Agile Flexibility with Strategic Consistency

While agility is about responsiveness to change, maintaining a strategic focus ensures that efforts are not dispersed and that the organization moves in a coherent direction.

- **Flexible Yet Focused Roadmaps**: Develop strategic roadmaps that outline critical objectives but are flexible enough to allow for pivoting when necessary. This ensures that while the organization remains agile, it does not deviate from its core strategic goals.

- **Dynamic Resource Allocation**: Adapt resource allocation dynamically to balance between maintaining core systems and investing in innovative projects. This strategy ensures that resources are used efficiently and can be reallocated in response to shifting priorities.

- **Strategic Innovation Portfolios**: Manage a portfolio of projects that includes both core development and innovation initiatives. This portfolio management approach helps maintain a balance between exploiting existing assets and exploring new opportunities.

By employing these advanced strategies to maintain flexibility and foster innovation, technology and architecture leaders can ensure that their Agile projects are both adaptable and aligned with long-term strategic goals. These practices not only support ongoing project requirements but also prepare the organization to meet future challenges and opportunities effectively.

Chapter 7: Stakeholder Engagement in Agile Environments

Successful Agile projects require more than just skilled teams and robust processes—they demand strong and consistent stakeholder engagement. Stakeholders play a critical role in shaping project goals, validating progress, and ensuring alignment with broader business objectives. In Agile environments, where requirements evolve and feedback is continuous, effectively managing stakeholder relationships is essential for delivering value and maintaining trust.

Engaging stakeholders in Agile projects involves more than periodic updates; it requires active collaboration and transparent communication. Stakeholders must feel empowered to contribute their perspectives and see how their input influences the project's direction. At the same time, Agile teams must balance competing stakeholder priorities, navigate conflicts, and foster alignment across diverse interests.

This chapter explores strategies for effective stakeholder engagement in Agile environments. From understanding stakeholder needs and tailoring communication to involving them in Agile processes and overcoming challenges, this chapter provides actionable insights to build strong partnerships. By mastering stakeholder engagement, teams can ensure that their projects deliver meaningful value while cultivating lasting relationships.

Understanding Stakeholder Needs in Agile Projects

Stakeholders are integral to the success of Agile projects. Their needs, expectations, and feedback guide the team's direction, ensuring the final deliverable aligns with strategic goals and user requirements. This section explores how Agile teams can identify stakeholders effectively, understand their dynamic needs, and prioritize engagement to achieve maximum alignment and project success.

Identifying Stakeholders

The first step in effective stakeholder engagement is identifying all relevant parties who influence or are affected by the project. Stakeholders typically fall into internal and external categories, each with unique needs and expectations.

- **Internal Stakeholders**:
    - **Executive Leadership**: Define strategic goals and allocate resources. Their priorities often revolve around ROI, compliance, and alignment with the organization's vision.
    - **Team Members**: Include developers, designers, testers, and product owners who directly contribute to the project. Their focus is on clarity of requirements, tools, and achievable goals.
- **External Stakeholders**:
    - **Customers/End-Users**: Represent the ultimate consumers of the product or service. Their priorities include usability, functionality, and satisfaction.

- o **Regulators and Partners**: External agencies or business partners who may impose specific standards or contribute to the project's ecosystem.

Techniques for Stakeholder Identification:

- **Stakeholder Mapping**: Use tools such as a stakeholder map to visually represent all stakeholders, their roles, and their level of influence.

- **Brainstorming Sessions**: Conduct cross-departmental brainstorming sessions to identify overlooked stakeholders, ensuring inclusivity.

- **Stakeholder Interviews**: Engage with leaders from various departments or external partners to ensure a comprehensive understanding of the stakeholder landscape.

Understanding Dynamic Stakeholder Expectations

Agile projects thrive on their ability to adapt to change, which includes evolving stakeholder expectations. Regularly assessing these expectations ensures alignment and minimizes friction during the project lifecycle.

- **Dynamic Needs Analysis**: Stakeholder expectations are rarely static. Agile teams must establish processes to regularly assess these needs through tools such as:

  - o **Dynamic Roadmaps**: Create roadmaps that evolve based on feedback and shifting priorities.

  - o **Personas and Empathy Maps**: Build detailed personas for key stakeholders to understand their goals, pain points, and motivations better.

- **Segmentation of Stakeholders**:

  - o **High-Interest, High-Influence Stakeholders**: Engage these stakeholders regularly, ensuring their expectations align with the project's direction.

  - o **Low-Interest, Low-Influence Stakeholders**: Keep informed through periodic updates to maintain goodwill and awareness.

Practical Applications:

- **Feedback-Driven Refinements**: Gather input through sprint reviews and user testing sessions to adjust deliverables to better meet stakeholder needs.

- **Proactive Expectation Management**: Use scenario planning to anticipate potential changes in stakeholder priorities and prepare contingency strategies.

Prioritizing Stakeholder Engagement

In Agile environments, where time and resources are limited, prioritizing stakeholder engagement is crucial to ensure the team focuses on high-impact interactions.

- **Prioritization Frameworks**:

  - o **Power-Interest Grid**: Classify stakeholders based on their level of influence and interest. For example:

- High Power, High Interest: Actively engage through regular meetings and updates.

- Low Power, Low Interest: Keep informed with minimal engagement.

- **RACI Matrix**: Define stakeholder roles and responsibilities using the Responsible, Accountable, Consulted, and Informed framework.

- **Customized Engagement Strategies**:

  - Tailor communication methods to each stakeholder group. For example:

    - Executives may prefer high-level dashboards or quarterly reports.

    - End-users may benefit from more hands-on engagement, such as usability testing and focus groups.

Case Example: A Tech Startup's Stakeholder Mapping Process

A fast-growing tech startup developing a new SaaS platform struggled to align its teams with the needs of diverse stakeholders. By implementing a robust stakeholder mapping process, the startup identified three key groups: investors, enterprise customers, and regulatory agencies. Using personas and empathy maps, the team tailored its engagement approach:

- **Investors**: Provided high-level updates and ROI projections through monthly reports.

- **Enterprise Customers**: Organized workshops and focus groups to gather input on features and usability.

- **Regulatory Agencies**: Scheduled regular check-ins to ensure compliance, avoiding costly delays.

This focused approach resulted in faster iterations, improved customer satisfaction, and a smooth product launch.

Understanding stakeholder needs is the foundation of effective engagement in Agile projects. By identifying stakeholders comprehensively, analyzing their evolving expectations, and prioritizing their engagement strategically, Agile teams can align their efforts with organizational goals and user needs. This foundational work not only minimizes friction but also fosters collaboration and trust throughout the project lifecycle.

Communicating with Stakeholders in Agile Projects

Effective communication is the backbone of stakeholder engagement in Agile projects. It ensures alignment between the team's deliverables and the stakeholders' expectations while fostering trust and collaboration. This section explores advanced communication strategies, tools, and practices that Agile teams can use to engage stakeholders effectively, navigate conflicts, and promote transparency.

Advanced Communication Strategies

Tailoring communication approaches to different stakeholder groups is critical in Agile environments where stakeholders have varying levels of interest, influence, and technical expertise.

- **Stakeholder-Specific Communication**:

  - **Executives and Sponsors**: Focus on high-level updates, such as progress against strategic goals, ROI, and risk management. Use concise reports, dashboards, or presentations that emphasize impact and outcomes.

  - **End-Users and Customers**: Prioritize detailed discussions around product features, usability, and feedback. Engage them through prototypes, demonstrations, and usability testing.

  - **Regulators and Partners**: Provide technical and compliance-focused information, ensuring transparency and adherence to relevant standards.

- **Two-Way Communication**:

  - Establish mechanisms that allow stakeholders to voice concerns, provide input, and influence project direction. This can include:

    - **Feedback Loops**: Regular feedback sessions during sprint reviews or retrospectives.

    - **Surveys and Polls**: Periodic surveys to gather stakeholder opinions on key project aspects.

  - Ensure stakeholders feel heard by demonstrating how their feedback has been incorporated into project decisions.

Using Collaborative Tools

Digital tools play a crucial role in enhancing communication, especially in distributed or hybrid teams where face-to-face interaction is limited.

- **Project Management Platforms**: Tools like Jira, Trello, or Asana provide transparency by visualizing project progress, backlogs, and workflows. These platforms allow stakeholders to monitor updates in real time.

- **Collaboration Software**: Platforms like Slack, Microsoft Teams, and Zoom facilitate real-time communication and asynchronous discussions. Create dedicated channels for specific stakeholders to keep communication streamlined.

- **Documentation and Sharing Tools**: Use tools like Confluence, Google Drive, or Notion to create centralized repositories for project documentation, meeting notes, and decisions. This ensures stakeholders have easy access to the latest information.

Case Example: A distributed Agile team at a global e-commerce company used Miro to conduct virtual sprint planning sessions with stakeholders. The interactive whiteboard allowed for real-time collaboration and alignment, reducing misunderstandings and ensuring everyone was on the same page.

Conflict Management and Negotiation

In Agile environments, conflicts between stakeholders are inevitable due to differing priorities, resource constraints, and evolving project scopes. Effectively managing these conflicts is critical to maintaining alignment and momentum.

- **Identifying the Root Cause**:
  - Use active listening and open-ended questions to uncover the underlying reasons for stakeholder disagreements. Often, conflicts arise due to misaligned expectations or inadequate communication.

- **Facilitating Collaborative Discussions**:
  - Agile leaders can act as mediators, ensuring all stakeholders have an opportunity to express their concerns. Techniques include:
    - **Consensus-Building Workshops**: Bring stakeholders together to discuss differing viewpoints and collaboratively arrive at a resolution.
    - **Interest-Based Negotiation**: Focus on the shared goals and interests of all parties rather than positions or demands.

- **Escalation Protocols**:
  - Establish clear protocols for resolving escalated conflicts. This may involve bringing in senior leaders or neutral third parties to mediate and provide direction.

Case Example: During the development of a fintech app, conflicting priorities arose between compliance teams (focused on security) and product managers (pushing for faster time-to-market). The Agile team organized a facilitated workshop to prioritize tasks that balanced security requirements with market demands, resulting in a mutually agreeable roadmap.

Visual Communication and Transparency

Visual tools enhance clarity and engagement, especially when conveying complex information to stakeholders with varying levels of technical expertise.

- **Kanban Boards**: Provide a clear visual representation of project workflows, enabling stakeholders to track task statuses at a glance.

- **Dashboards**: Use dashboards to present key metrics such as sprint velocity, budget utilization, and progress toward milestones. Ensure dashboards are customized to meet the needs of different stakeholder groups.

- **Prototypes and Mockups**: For end-users and customers, prototypes and interactive mockups are invaluable in demonstrating progress and gathering actionable feedback.

Case Example: A software development team used Power BI to create a live dashboard for executives overseeing a major project. The dashboard included KPIs on project progress, risk levels, and resource allocation, ensuring that executives stayed informed without needing frequent detailed meetings.

Building Long-Term Trust Through Communication

Consistent and transparent communication builds trust, a cornerstone of successful stakeholder engagement.

- **Regular Check-Ins**:

- Schedule recurring meetings with stakeholders to review progress, address concerns, and discuss upcoming priorities. Use sprint reviews and retrospectives to formalize these check-ins.

- **Transparency in Challenges**:

  - Be upfront about risks, delays, or challenges. Stakeholders are more likely to remain supportive when they are informed early and presented with proposed solutions.

- **Demonstrating Results**:

  - Highlight tangible outcomes of stakeholder contributions. For instance, show how user feedback directly influenced product design or how executive input shaped the project's strategic alignment.

Effective communication is at the heart of stakeholder engagement in Agile projects. By employing advanced communication strategies, leveraging collaborative tools, managing conflicts constructively, and emphasizing transparency, Agile teams can foster trust and alignment with stakeholders. This ensures that projects not only meet their objectives but also maintain strong, supportive relationships with all involved parties.

Involving Stakeholders in the Agile Process

Involving stakeholders in the Agile process is essential to ensuring alignment between project goals and stakeholder expectations. When stakeholders actively participate, they gain a deeper understanding of the Agile approach and contribute valuable insights that enhance the project's success. This section explores effective methods for engaging stakeholders, balancing their involvement, and fostering ownership throughout the Agile lifecycle.

Stakeholder Participation in Agile Ceremonies

Agile ceremonies provide structured opportunities to involve stakeholders at various stages of the project. Their participation ensures that deliverables remain aligned with stakeholder needs while enhancing transparency and collaboration.

In sprint planning meetings, stakeholders can offer critical input on prioritizing backlog items based on their strategic value or business impact. This collaborative approach ensures that the team focuses on high-priority features, maximizing value delivery. During sprint reviews, stakeholders can evaluate progress, provide feedback, and suggest adjustments to keep the project aligned with its objectives. These sessions offer a platform for stakeholders to voice concerns and see how their contributions shape the outcome.

Retrospectives also benefit from stakeholder participation. While typically internal, inviting key stakeholders occasionally can provide external perspectives on process improvements and areas for collaboration enhancement. This fosters a sense of shared ownership and helps build trust between the team and stakeholders.

Balancing Stakeholder Interests and Input

Agile projects often involve multiple stakeholders with differing priorities and expectations. Balancing these interests requires a structured approach to ensure that no single voice dominates the process while all relevant inputs are considered.

A clear framework for managing stakeholder contributions is essential. The Responsible, Accountable, Consulted, and Informed (RACI) matrix is an effective tool for defining roles and responsibilities, ensuring that each stakeholder understands their involvement in decision-making processes. For instance, while product owners may be responsible for prioritizing the backlog, end-users can be consulted to validate user stories or test prototypes.

Facilitated workshops can also be used to mediate competing interests. These workshops provide a neutral environment for stakeholders to discuss their priorities, identify shared goals, and reach a consensus. Establishing shared objectives during these sessions can help align diverse stakeholder groups toward a common vision.

Building Stakeholder Buy-In and Ownership

Stakeholder buy-in is critical to the success of Agile projects. When stakeholders feel a sense of ownership, they are more likely to actively support the project and contribute constructively to its outcomes.

One way to foster ownership is through co-creation workshops, where stakeholders and Agile teams collaborate to define requirements, create user stories, or design solutions. This hands-on involvement empowers stakeholders, making them invested in the project's success. For example, inviting end-users to participate in usability testing sessions not only validates the product but also strengthens their connection to its development.

Transparency is another key factor in building trust and ownership. Regularly share progress updates, challenges, and decision rationales with stakeholders. This open communication reinforces their confidence in the team's capabilities and ensures they remain informed and engaged throughout the project.

Finally, recognize and celebrate stakeholder contributions. Publicly acknowledging their role in the project's achievements can motivate stakeholders to remain actively involved and advocate for the Agile approach within their organizations.

Case Example

Stakeholder Engagement in a Government IT Project

A government IT project aimed at digitizing citizen services faced challenges in aligning the priorities of various departments. To address this, the project team implemented a comprehensive stakeholder engagement strategy. Stakeholders from finance, legal, and public services were invited to sprint planning and review meetings. This allowed each department to articulate its requirements and validate progress in real-time.

The team also conducted co-creation workshops to develop user-friendly interfaces, incorporating feedback from citizens, civil servants, and technical staff. This collaborative approach ensured that the final product met diverse needs while fostering a sense of ownership among all participants. The project's success demonstrated how active stakeholder involvement could bridge departmental silos and deliver a solution that exceeded expectations.

Involving stakeholders in the Agile process is about more than just inviting them to meetings. It requires deliberate efforts to engage them meaningfully, balance competing interests, and foster a sense of shared ownership. By integrating stakeholders into Agile ceremonies, managing their input strategically, and emphasizing transparency and recognition, teams can build strong partnerships that drive project success and create long-lasting value.

Addressing Challenges in Stakeholder Engagement

Engaging stakeholders effectively in Agile environments is not without its challenges. Different priorities, resistance to change, communication barriers, and conflicts of interest can hinder the success of stakeholder relationships. This section addresses these common challenges and provides practical solutions to ensure effective and constructive stakeholder engagement throughout the Agile process.

Overcoming Resistance to Agile Practices

Resistance to Agile practices is one of the most frequent challenges encountered when engaging stakeholders. This resistance often stems from a lack of understanding about Agile methodologies or a reluctance to shift away from traditional processes.

To overcome this resistance, begin by educating stakeholders on the benefits of Agile. Conduct workshops, presentations, or one-on-one sessions to demystify Agile concepts, focusing on how Agile practices deliver better results through collaboration, iterative development, and adaptability. Tailor these discussions to the concerns of specific stakeholder groups. For example, executives might be more interested in how Agile improves ROI and risk management, while team members may value insights on how Agile simplifies workflows and enhances job satisfaction.

Involve stakeholders early in the Agile transition process. When they are part of the planning and implementation phases, they are more likely to feel a sense of ownership and alignment with Agile principles. Additionally, highlight small wins and incremental successes throughout the project to demonstrate how Agile practices are driving value. These examples can build confidence and gradually reduce resistance.

Engaging Remote and Global Stakeholders

In today's interconnected world, Agile projects often involve stakeholders who are geographically dispersed, working across different time zones, and from diverse cultural backgrounds. Engaging remote and global stakeholders presents unique challenges that require thoughtful strategies to address.

To manage time zone differences effectively, implement a combination of synchronous and asynchronous communication methods. Schedule recurring meetings at times that accommodate as many stakeholders as possible, rotating the schedule if needed to share the inconvenience. For asynchronous updates, use digital tools like Slack, Microsoft Teams, or project management platforms to share progress, gather feedback, and maintain transparency.

Cultural differences may also create misunderstandings or misalignments in expectations. Take the time to understand the cultural norms and communication styles of your stakeholders. Be sensitive to varying levels of formality, decision-making approaches, and comfort with conflict resolution. Encourage team members to develop cultural competency through training and provide translators or cultural liaisons when necessary for smoother collaboration.

Building trust with remote stakeholders is crucial. Use video calls and face-to-face meetings when possible to establish rapport. Consistent follow-ups, clear documentation, and honoring commitments also help reinforce trust in virtual and global contexts.

Navigating Conflicts Among Stakeholders

Conflicts are inevitable in Agile projects, especially when stakeholders have competing priorities or differing visions for the project. Left unresolved, these conflicts can stall progress and damage relationships.

To navigate conflicts effectively, begin by understanding the root cause. Use active listening techniques to give stakeholders the opportunity to share their perspectives and underlying concerns. This can uncover hidden interests that may not be immediately apparent but are critical to finding a resolution.

Facilitate structured discussions to explore potential solutions collaboratively. Techniques like brainstorming sessions or fishbone diagrams can help identify creative ways to address conflicts. When mediating, emphasize shared goals and the mutual benefits of resolving the conflict. For example, remind stakeholders that delivering a high-quality product on time serves everyone's interests.

In situations where consensus cannot be reached, escalate the issue to senior leadership or a neutral third party who can make an objective decision. Establishing clear escalation protocols early in the project ensures that conflicts are handled efficiently without derailing progress.

Real-World Example

Managing Stakeholder Engagement Challenges

A large multinational company developing a new supply chain management platform faced significant challenges in aligning its diverse stakeholder groups. The IT department prioritized technical feasibility, while business units focused on usability and rapid deployment. Additionally, external logistics partners demanded specific integrations that were outside the project's original scope.

To address these issues, the company established a stakeholder advisory board, bringing representatives from each group together regularly to discuss priorities and negotiate compromises. They used collaborative tools like shared dashboards to provide real-time visibility into progress and task ownership. A dedicated Agile coach facilitated discussions to ensure that everyone's perspectives were considered while keeping the project aligned with its overall objectives.

By fostering open communication and prioritizing transparency, the company resolved conflicts, strengthened relationships among stakeholders, and delivered a platform that met both technical and business needs.

Building Stakeholder Trust

Trust is the foundation of successful stakeholder engagement. Agile teams must prioritize transparency, reliability, and accountability to build and maintain trust.

Being transparent involves sharing both successes and challenges. Stakeholders are more likely to remain supportive when they are informed about risks, delays, or roadblocks early, accompanied by proposed solutions. Demonstrating reliability means following through on commitments, such as delivering updates, providing reports, or completing agreed-upon tasks. Accountability requires owning mistakes and taking corrective actions promptly, further reinforcing trust.

Recognize and respect stakeholder contributions. Publicly acknowledge their input and show how it has influenced project decisions or deliverables. This not only validates their involvement but also fosters a deeper sense of partnership.

Engaging stakeholders in Agile projects involves addressing a wide array of challenges, from resistance to change to conflicts and communication barriers. By implementing proactive strategies, fostering collaboration, and emphasizing trust, Agile teams can transform these challenges into opportunities to strengthen stakeholder relationships. Effective engagement ensures alignment, fosters collaboration, and ultimately drives project success.

Measuring Stakeholder Engagement Success

Measuring the effectiveness of stakeholder engagement is crucial for ensuring that Agile projects align with stakeholder expectations and deliver value. Without concrete metrics and systematic evaluation, it can be challenging to determine whether engagement efforts are achieving the desired outcomes. This section explores strategies for tracking and measuring stakeholder engagement success, focusing on actionable metrics, the use of feedback loops, and methods for fostering continuous improvement.

Defining Metrics for Stakeholder Engagement

The first step in measuring stakeholder engagement is to establish clear, relevant metrics that reflect the goals of the engagement process. These metrics should align with both project objectives and stakeholder expectations.

- **Stakeholder Satisfaction**: Measure satisfaction levels through surveys or feedback forms after key meetings, sprint reviews, or project milestones. Questions can gauge stakeholders' perceptions of transparency, collaboration, and alignment with their priorities.

- **Engagement Participation Rates**: Track attendance and active participation in Agile ceremonies such as sprint planning, reviews, and retrospectives. Low participation may indicate disengagement, while consistent involvement suggests strong engagement.

- **Timeliness and Responsiveness**: Monitor how quickly stakeholders respond to project updates, feedback requests, or decision-making opportunities. A high response rate signals strong involvement, while delays may highlight potential engagement issues.

- **Quality of Feedback**: Assess the depth and relevance of feedback provided by stakeholders. Effective engagement often leads to actionable, specific feedback that directly improves project deliverables.

- **Alignment Metrics**: Evaluate how well the final deliverables align with the stakeholders' initial objectives and priorities. This can be assessed through stakeholder reviews, goal achievement analysis, and post-project evaluations.

Implementing Feedback Loops

Feedback loops are essential for continuously refining stakeholder engagement practices. They allow teams to gather insights, adjust strategies, and foster stronger relationships over time.

- **Regular Stakeholder Check-Ins**: Schedule periodic meetings with stakeholders to review progress, discuss challenges, and gather feedback. Use these sessions to identify areas where engagement practices can be improved.

- **Real-Time Feedback Mechanisms**: Utilize digital tools like Slack, Microsoft Teams, or survey platforms to collect real-time feedback from stakeholders during and after Agile ceremonies.

- **Anonymous Feedback Options**: Offer anonymous feedback channels to encourage stakeholders to share honest opinions, particularly about sensitive issues. This can provide valuable insights into hidden concerns or barriers to engagement.

Continuous Improvement Strategies

Stakeholder engagement is not a static process; it should evolve based on feedback and changing project dynamics. Agile principles of iteration and adaptation can be applied to improve engagement over time.

- **Analyze Engagement Data**: Regularly review engagement metrics and feedback to identify trends and areas for improvement. For example, if participation in sprint reviews is declining, investigate the root cause and implement corrective measures, such as adjusting meeting formats or schedules.

- **Iterative Engagement Practices**: Experiment with new engagement strategies, such as co-creation workshops, enhanced communication tools, or rotating stakeholder roles in Agile ceremonies. Evaluate the effectiveness of these initiatives and refine them based on stakeholder feedback.

- **Recognition and Acknowledgment**: Highlight and reward positive stakeholder contributions to the project. Recognizing active and constructive engagement fosters goodwill and encourages continued participation.

Examples of Measuring Engagement Success

To illustrate how these strategies can be implemented, consider the following examples:

1. **Technology Startup**: A startup developing a new mobile app tracked stakeholder engagement using satisfaction surveys after each sprint review. The team identified that stakeholders valued more detailed demonstrations of progress, leading to the addition of live demos in subsequent reviews, which increased satisfaction scores by 25%.

2. **Government Agency**: A government agency used participation rates and feedback forms to assess stakeholder engagement in a digital transformation project. Low participation in sprint planning sessions revealed scheduling conflicts. By offering flexible meeting times and asynchronous input options, the agency improved attendance by 40%.

3. **Retail Chain**: A global retailer introduced anonymous surveys to gather stakeholder opinions on the Agile process. Feedback indicated that stakeholders desired more clarity on how their input was being implemented. The retailer responded by creating a feedback tracker that showed the status of stakeholder suggestions, resulting in higher transparency and stronger trust.

Measuring stakeholder engagement success is an ongoing process that requires thoughtful metrics, robust feedback loops, and a commitment to continuous improvement. By defining relevant metrics, gathering actionable feedback, and iterating on engagement practices, Agile teams can build stronger relationships with stakeholders, ensure alignment with project goals, and enhance overall project outcomes. Stakeholder engagement is not just about involvement but about creating a partnership that drives mutual success.

Chapter 8: Risk Management in Agile Projects

Every project involves risk, but in the dynamic and fast-paced world of Agile, managing those risks effectively becomes even more critical. Agile projects, with their iterative cycles and emphasis on adaptability, offer unique opportunities to identify, analyze, and mitigate risks throughout the development process. However, this requires a proactive approach to risk management, seamlessly integrated into Agile workflows.

Risk management in Agile projects goes beyond traditional practices of identifying risks upfront and addressing them later. Instead, it emphasizes continuous risk assessment, collaboration across teams, and the use of iterative feedback loops to adapt to emerging challenges. Agile's flexibility provides an inherent advantage in responding to risks, allowing teams to pivot quickly when necessary.

This chapter explores the principles and practices of risk management in Agile environments. From identifying risks early and developing mitigation strategies to embedding risk management in Agile ceremonies and leveraging metrics for tracking progress, this chapter provides a comprehensive guide for reducing uncertainty and ensuring project success. By mastering Agile risk management, leaders can build resilience into their teams and deliver high-quality outcomes, even in the face of complexity and change.

Understanding Risk in Agile Environments

Effective risk management is crucial in Agile projects, where the flexibility and speed of the development process can expose projects to various risks. Understanding how to identify and assess these risks is foundational to maintaining project integrity and success. This section explores the common types of risks associated with Agile projects and introduces methodologies for assessing the impact and likelihood of these risks.

Identifying Risks in Agile Projects

Agile projects, with their iterative nature and emphasis on rapid deployment, face unique risks. Identifying these risks early and accurately is crucial for mitigating potential negative impacts on the project.

- **Scope Creep**: Unlike traditional project management, Agile projects can be particularly susceptible to scope creep due to their iterative nature and frequent reassessments. This risk can lead to dilution of project goals and misallocation of resources.

- **Technological Risks**: Agile projects often employ cutting-edge technologies that can be unstable or poorly documented. This adoption can introduce risks related to tool integration, performance issues, and dependency on external vendors or technologies.

- **Resource Fluctuations**: Given the dynamic work environments in which Agile projects operate, they can often face risks related to resource availability, including fluctuations in team composition and challenges in skill alignment.

- **Stakeholder Engagement**: Agile requires active and ongoing stakeholder engagement. Inconsistent stakeholder participation can lead to misaligned expectations and deliverables that do not fully meet user needs.

Tools and Techniques for Risk Identification

To systematically identify risks in Agile projects, several tools and techniques can be employed:

- **Risk Workshops and Brainstorming Sessions**: Conduct regular risk identification workshops involving the project team and stakeholders to brainstorm potential risks based on their expertise and project experience.

- **Checklists and Templates**: Utilize risk identification checklists tailored to Agile projects to ensure all common risk areas are considered during the planning and execution phases.

- **User Stories and Use Cases**: Analyze user stories and use cases to identify potential failure points and operational risks that could impact the functionality and usability of the deliverable.

Assessing Risk Impact and Likelihood

Once risks are identified, assessing their impact and likelihood is critical for prioritizing risk management efforts effectively.

- **Risk Matrices**: Use risk matrices to categorize risks based on their potential impact and likelihood. This tool helps in visualizing which risks require immediate attention and which may be monitored over time.

- **Qualitative Assessments**: Engage with project teams and stakeholders in qualitative assessments to gain insights into the potential consequences of identified risks. These assessments can help in understanding the nuances of how certain risks may affect project outcomes differently.

- **Quantitative Methods**: Where possible, apply quantitative methods such as Monte Carlo simulations or probabilistic modeling to assess risk impact. These methods are particularly useful in understanding the range of potential outcomes and the likelihood of different risk scenarios.

Importance of Early and Continuous Risk Assessment

- **Early Detection**: Early detection allows teams to implement mitigation strategies before risks can have a significant impact, preserving resources and keeping the project on track.

- **Continuous Assessment**: Agile projects benefit from continuous risk assessment due to their iterative nature. Each iteration provides an opportunity to reassess existing risks and identify new ones, adapting risk management strategies in real time.

Understanding and effectively managing risks in Agile environments are crucial for the success of projects. By employing systematic identification and assessment strategies, teams can anticipate potential problems and take proactive steps to mitigate them, ensuring that the project remains resilient and adaptable.

Agile Strategies for Risk Mitigation

Once risks have been identified and assessed in Agile projects, the next crucial step is implementing effective mitigation strategies. This part of the chapter explores proactive techniques and cultural practices that enhance risk management in Agile environments, focusing on maintaining project momentum while minimizing negative impacts.

Proactive Risk Mitigation Techniques

In Agile project management, being proactive about risk mitigation is essential. By implementing these techniques early and iteratively, teams can address risks before they become issues that threaten project success.

- **Iterative Testing**: Agile projects benefit from continuous integration and testing, which can help identify and resolve issues early in the development cycle. This approach allows teams to address small issues before they evolve into larger problems.

- **Feature Toggles**: Use feature toggles to manage and mitigate risks associated with releasing new features. This technique allows teams to enable or disable features dynamically without deploying new code, facilitating easier rollback and faster adjustments based on feedback.

- **Risk-Based Spike Solutions**: Implement spike solutions to explore potential risk areas or solutions to complex problems. Spikes are time-boxed investigations used to gain knowledge or solve specific, risk-related issues, helping to inform decision-making and refine project direction.

- **Automated Rollbacks and Recovery Strategies**: Develop automated systems for quick rollback in case new deployments fail. These strategies ensure that systems can be returned to a stable state without significant downtime, minimizing the impact on end-users.

Building a Risk-Responsive Culture

Creating a culture that understands and effectively responds to risks is pivotal in Agile environments. This involves not just processes and tools but also attitudes and behaviors that prioritize risk management.

- **Training and Awareness**: Regular training sessions on risk management practices and tools can empower team members to recognize and respond to risks proactively. Awareness campaigns can help embed risk management into the daily workflow of teams.

- **Empowerment and Accountability**: Empower team members to take ownership of risks in their areas of work. This includes giving them the authority to make decisions and take actions that mitigate risks without waiting for higher-level approvals.

- **Open Communication Channels**: Foster an environment where team members feel comfortable reporting potential risks and challenges. Open communication channels help ensure that issues are addressed promptly and collaboratively.

Integrating Risk Management in Agile Ceremonies

Agile ceremonies provide structured opportunities for teams to discuss, assess, and plan risk mitigation strategies. Integrating risk management into these ceremonies can enhance visibility and collective responsibility.

- **Sprint Planning**: Incorporate risk assessment into sprint planning sessions. Discuss potential risks for each task or story and plan mitigation actions as part of the sprint commitments.

- **Daily Stand-Ups**: Use daily stand-ups to quickly identify and communicate new risks and updates on ongoing risk mitigation efforts. This daily check-in helps keep risk management front and center in team activities.

- **Sprint Retrospectives**: Dedicate part of each retrospective to discuss what risks were encountered, how they were handled, and what improvements can be made to risk management practices in future sprints.

Continuous Improvement of Risk Management Practices

Agile is all about continuous improvement—not just in product development but also in processes, including risk management.

- **Feedback Loops**: Establish feedback loops specifically for risk management processes. Gather feedback on the effectiveness of risk mitigation strategies and integrate this feedback into process improvements.

- **Metrics and KPIs for Risk Management**: Define key performance indicators (KPIs) related to risk management, such as the number of risks mitigated, average time to mitigate risks, and impacts of risks on project timelines or budgets. Use these metrics to track performance and guide improvements.

Proactive risk mitigation strategies and a risk-responsive culture are integral to the success of Agile projects. By embedding risk management into Agile practices and ceremonies and fostering a culture that prioritizes addressing risks, teams can not only minimize the impacts of potential issues but also enhance the overall resilience and success of projects.

Implementing and Monitoring Risk Controls

Effective risk management in Agile projects extends beyond the identification and initial mitigation of risks. It also involves the careful implementation of risk controls and the ongoing monitoring of their effectiveness. This section explores how Agile teams can develop, implement, and continuously monitor risk controls to ensure that project risks are managed dynamically and efficiently throughout the project lifecycle.

Developing and Implementing Risk Controls

Risk controls in Agile projects need to be flexible and adaptable, allowing for rapid response to changing project conditions and new risks. The development and implementation of these controls must be integrated into the Agile workflow to maintain project momentum and effectiveness.

- **Risk Control Strategies**: Define specific strategies for each identified risk, detailing how the risk will be managed, mitigated, or avoided. Strategies may include preemptive actions, contingency plans, or avoidance techniques.

- **Integration into Project Plans**: Incorporate risk controls into the project planning process. For Agile projects, this means embedding risk management actions into sprint planning and backlog prioritization, ensuring that risk mitigation is treated as part of the regular workflow.

- **Tools and Automation**: Leverage technology to automate risk controls where possible. This can include automated monitoring tools that track performance metrics and trigger alerts when risk thresholds are exceeded. Automation helps ensure that risk controls are consistently applied and reduces the likelihood of human error.

Monitoring and Adjusting Risk Controls

The dynamic nature of Agile projects requires that risk controls be monitored continuously and adjusted as necessary. This adaptability is crucial to the success of risk management efforts in an Agile environment.

- **Regular Risk Reviews**: Schedule regular risk review sessions as part of Agile ceremonies, such as during sprint reviews or retrospectives. Use these opportunities to assess the effectiveness of risk controls and make necessary adjustments.

- **Real-time Monitoring Tools**: Implement real-time monitoring tools that provide ongoing visibility into risk metrics. Tools that integrate with Agile project management software can offer dashboards that update with the latest risk data, helping teams stay informed about potential issues.

- **Feedback Mechanisms**: Establish robust feedback mechanisms that allow team members to report on the effectiveness of risk controls and suggest improvements. This feedback can be collected through direct communication channels, digital platforms, or regular surveys.

Examples of Effective Risk Controls in Agile

To illustrate the application of these concepts, consider the following examples of how risk controls have been successfully implemented and monitored in Agile projects:

- **Example 1: Financial Services App Development**
  - **Risk**: Security vulnerabilities in new features.
  - **Control Implementation**: Integration of automated security testing into the continuous integration/continuous deployment (CI/CD) pipeline.
  - **Monitoring**: Automated alerts and regular security audit reports to monitor the effectiveness of security measures.
  - **Adjustment**: Rapid iteration on security protocols based on the latest threat intelligence and feedback from security audits.

- **Example 2: E-commerce Platform Scaling**

- **Risk**: Performance bottlenecks under high user load.

- **Control Implementation**: Implementation of performance testing sprints that simulate increased traffic.

- **Monitoring**: Use of performance monitoring tools that track response times and system stability.

- **Adjustment**: Adjustments to system architecture and resource allocation based on performance data and user feedback.

Implementing and monitoring risk controls in Agile projects is a continuous process that requires integration into the Agile cycle of planning, action, review, and adaptation. By developing tailored risk controls, leveraging technology for monitoring, and fostering an environment of continuous feedback, Agile teams can effectively manage project risks, ensuring resilience and success.

Learning from Risk and Failures

In Agile methodologies, learning from risks and failures is not just about recovery; it's an opportunity to enhance future project performance and build a more resilient organization. This section explores how Agile teams can capture lessons from their experiences with risks and failures and use these insights to strengthen their project management practices and risk mitigation strategies.

Capturing Lessons Learned

Continuous improvement is a core principle of Agile, and capturing lessons learned from both successful and unsuccessful risk mitigation efforts is essential for this process.

- **Structured Retrospectives for Risk Analysis**: Incorporate specific discussions about risks and failures into regular retrospective meetings. Encourage teams to analyze what went wrong, what worked, and how similar risks can be better managed in the future. Documenting these discussions ensures that valuable insights are preserved and accessible for future reference.

- **Creating a Knowledge Base**: Develop a centralized repository where all lessons learned, risk logs, and retrospective outcomes are stored. This knowledge base should be searchable and categorized to help teams quickly find relevant information for similar future situations.

- **Case Study Development**: Write detailed case studies on significant risk events or failures and how they were handled. These case studies can be used for training purposes and to help new team members understand the typical risks associated with projects and the preferred approaches to managing them.

Implementing Continuous Improvement Loops

Agile projects thrive on feedback and the continuous iteration of processes. Implementing continuous improvement loops specifically targeted at risk management can significantly enhance project outcomes over time.

- **Feedback Loops from Stakeholders**: Regularly solicit feedback from stakeholders on how risks are managed and involve them in the retrospective processes. Stakeholder perspectives can provide external insights that might not be apparent to project teams.

- **Adapting Risk Management Practices**: Use the insights gained from retrospectives and stakeholder feedback to refine risk management methodologies. This could involve updating risk assessment templates, adjusting risk thresholds, or introducing new tools and technologies for better risk monitoring.

- **Training and Development Programs**: Regularly update training programs to include new risk management strategies and lessons learned from past projects. Continuous learning should be promoted across the organization to ensure that all team members are equipped to handle project risks effectively.

Promoting a Culture of Risk Awareness and Proactivity

Fostering a culture that actively engages with risks rather than avoiding them can transform how an organization handles project challenges.

- **Rewarding Proactivity**: Recognize and reward team members who identify and mitigate risks early. Incentives can be aligned with risk management objectives to encourage a proactive approach across the team.

- **Open Discussions About Failures**: Create an environment where discussing failures is encouraged and not penalized. Open discussions about failures lead to a better understanding of risks and strengthen the team's ability to handle similar issues in the future.

- **Role of Leadership in Risk Culture**: Leadership should actively participate in risk management processes and demonstrate commitment to learning from risks and failures. Their involvement can help normalize the discussion around risks and encourage a more open, learning-focused approach across the organization.

Learning from risks and failures is integral to the Agile philosophy of continuous improvement. By systematically capturing lessons learned, implementing improvement loops, and fostering a culture that values proactive risk management, Agile teams can enhance their resilience and effectiveness. These practices not only mitigate the impacts of risks on current projects but also prepare teams to handle future challenges more competently.

Chapter 9: Quality Assurance and Testing Strategies

In Agile environments, quality is not an afterthought—it is a continuous and integral part of the development process. Agile Quality Assurance (QA) and testing strategies ensure that teams deliver high-quality software consistently, even in the face of rapid changes and tight timelines. By embedding QA into every stage of development, Agile teams can identify and address issues early, enhance collaboration, and deliver value with confidence.

Unlike traditional QA processes, which often occur at the end of the development cycle, Agile QA focuses on iterative testing, real-time feedback, and a collaborative approach to maintaining quality. Automated testing, continuous integration, and exploratory testing play pivotal roles in this approach, enabling teams to adapt quickly to changes without compromising on reliability or performance.

This chapter explores the principles, practices, and tools that underpin Agile QA and testing strategies. From foundational concepts to advanced techniques like Test-Driven Development (TDD) and Behavior-Driven Development (BDD), we explore how Agile teams can integrate quality into every aspect of their workflow. Whether scaling QA across multiple teams or preparing for emerging trends, this chapter provides a roadmap for maintaining excellence in software engineering and architecture.

Foundations of Agile QA and Testing

Quality Assurance (QA) plays a transformative role in Agile environments, going beyond traditional testing practices to become a continuous and integrated aspect of the software development lifecycle. In Agile, QA is not a separate phase; it is a collaborative process that ensures high-quality outcomes throughout development. This section explores the core principles of Agile QA and testing, the evolving role of QA in Agile teams, and the benefits it brings to software engineering and architecture.

Principles of Agile Testing

Agile testing is grounded in principles that align with the iterative, collaborative, and adaptive nature of Agile methodologies. These principles guide teams in embedding quality into every stage of the development process:

- **Test Early, Test Often**: Testing begins as early as the requirements phase and continues throughout the development lifecycle. Early testing identifies defects when they are cheaper and easier to fix, while continuous testing ensures ongoing quality.

- **Collaboration Between Developers and Testers**: In Agile teams, QA professionals work closely with developers, product owners, and other stakeholders. This collaboration fosters a shared understanding of quality and ensures that testing aligns with business goals.

- **Automation as a Core Practice**: Automated testing is an integral part of Agile QA. It accelerates feedback cycles, supports continuous integration and delivery, and reduces the time spent on repetitive tasks.

- **Continuous Improvement**: Agile teams regularly reflect on their testing processes during retrospectives, identifying areas for improvement and iterating on their QA strategies.

QA's Role in Agile Teams

The role of QA in Agile is significantly different from its role in traditional waterfall models. In Agile, QA professionals are embedded within cross-functional teams and contribute to all stages of development:

- **Early Involvement in Planning**: QA professionals participate in sprint planning sessions, helping to clarify requirements and identify potential risks early. This ensures that testing strategies are aligned with the team's objectives from the start.

- **Creating and Prioritizing Test Cases**: QA team members collaborate with product owners and developers to create test cases based on user stories. These test cases are prioritized alongside development tasks in the product backlog.

- **Acting as Quality Advocates**: Beyond finding defects, QA professionals advocate for quality throughout the project. They promote best practices, such as coding standards and test-driven development, and provide insights that help the team deliver a robust product.

Benefits of Agile QA

Agile QA offers significant advantages that enhance both product quality and team efficiency. These benefits make it an essential component of successful Agile projects:

- **Faster Feedback Loops**: Continuous testing provides rapid feedback on code changes, enabling teams to identify and resolve issues quickly. This accelerates development cycles and ensures higher-quality deliverables.

- **Improved Collaboration**: Agile QA fosters closer collaboration between testers, developers, and stakeholders, breaking down silos and creating a shared commitment to quality.

- **Higher Product Quality**: The iterative nature of Agile ensures that defects are caught and addressed incrementally, reducing the likelihood of critical issues in the final product.

- **Adaptability to Change**: Agile QA is inherently flexible, allowing teams to adapt their testing strategies to accommodate changing requirements and priorities.

Case Example

Early Testing in an E-Commerce Project

An e-commerce company implementing an Agile transformation used the principle of "test early, test often" to improve the quality of its website overhaul. By involving QA in sprint planning, the team identified potential usability issues during the design phase and created automated regression tests to ensure consistent functionality. As a result, the company reduced post-release defects by 40% and launched the new website two weeks ahead of schedule.

The foundations of Agile QA and testing lie in collaboration, iteration, and a proactive approach to quality. By embedding QA throughout the development lifecycle, teams can deliver high-quality products that meet user needs and adapt to changing requirements. These principles form the bedrock of Agile testing strategies and set the stage for more advanced techniques and tools explored in the next sections of this chapter.

Implementing Advanced Agile Testing Techniques

Agile environments demand testing techniques that align with their iterative, collaborative, and fast-paced nature. Advanced Agile testing methodologies such as Test-Driven Development (TDD), Behavior-Driven Development (BDD), and exploratory testing enable teams to maintain high standards of quality while adapting to evolving requirements. This section explores these techniques, providing detailed guidance on their implementation and value.

Test-Driven Development (TDD)

Test-Driven Development (TDD) is a practice where tests are written before the code itself. This approach ensures that each piece of code has a predefined purpose and is tested for functionality from the outset.

- **How TDD Works**:

    1. **Write a Test**: Before any code is written, create a test case that defines the desired functionality.

    2. **Run the Test**: Initially, the test will fail because the functionality does not yet exist.

    3. **Write the Code**: Develop the minimal amount of code required to pass the test.

    4. **Run the Test Again**: Ensure that the code passes the test.

    5. **Refactor the Code**: Optimize the code while ensuring it continues to pass the test.

- **Benefits of TDD**:

    o **Higher Code Quality**: Writing tests first ensures that all code is designed with testing in mind, resulting in cleaner, more maintainable code.

    o **Faster Debugging**: Since tests are written for every piece of functionality, identifying and fixing defects becomes significantly easier.

    o **Improved Collaboration**: TDD facilitates communication between developers, testers, and product owners by aligning the team on what the code should achieve.

- **Tools for TDD**:

    o **JUnit**: A widely used framework for unit testing in Java.

    o **RSpec**: A tool for behavior-driven development in Ruby that supports TDD principles.

- o **TestNG**: A testing framework for Java that integrates seamlessly with CI/CD pipelines.

Behavior-Driven Development (BDD)

Behavior-Driven Development (BDD) builds on the principles of TDD, focusing on the behavior of the software as defined by its stakeholders. It bridges the gap between technical and non-technical team members by using natural language to describe test cases.

- **How BDD Works**:
  - o BDD begins with creating feature files that describe application behavior in plain language. These files follow the "Given-When-Then" structure:
    - **Given**: Sets the context for the scenario.
    - **When**: Describes the action taken by the user.
    - **Then**: Outlines the expected outcome.
  - o Test cases written in this format are then automated using tools like Cucumber or SpecFlow.

- **Benefits of BDD**:
  - o **Stakeholder Collaboration**: BDD fosters collaboration between developers, testers, and business stakeholders by providing a shared language for discussing requirements.
  - o **Enhanced Requirements Clarity**: Writing behavior-driven tests ensures that all requirements are well-understood and explicitly documented.
  - o **Improved User Focus**: Since BDD scenarios are written from the end-user's perspective, it ensures that development efforts remain aligned with user needs.

- **Tools for BDD**:
  - o **Cucumber**: A popular BDD tool that supports multiple programming languages.
  - o **SpecFlow**: A BDD tool for .NET that integrates with Visual Studio.
  - o **Behat**: A BDD framework for PHP.

Exploratory Testing

Exploratory testing is a dynamic approach where testers actively explore the software to identify defects that automated tests may miss. Unlike scripted testing, exploratory testing is unscripted and relies on the tester's intuition and expertise.

- **How Exploratory Testing Works**:
  - o **Session-Based Testing**: Define time-boxed testing sessions with clear objectives (e.g., testing specific features or workflows).
  - o **Charter Creation**: Before starting, create a charter that outlines the scope, goals, and focus areas for the testing session.

- o **Documentation**: Record findings, including defects, observations, and questions, as the session progresses.

- **Benefits of Exploratory Testing**:

  - o **Uncovering Edge Cases**: Testers can identify unexpected defects and edge cases that scripted tests might overlook.

  - o **Enhancing Test Coverage**: Exploratory testing complements automated tests by providing an additional layer of coverage.

  - o **Adapting to Change**: This flexible approach allows testers to focus on areas that are most relevant as the software evolves.

- **Tools for Exploratory Testing**:

  - o **TestBuddy**: A tool designed for session-based exploratory testing.

  - o **qTest**: Provides exploratory testing features alongside traditional test management.

  - o **Session Tester**: Helps testers document exploratory testing sessions effectively.

Combining Advanced Testing Techniques

Agile teams often achieve the best results by combining multiple testing techniques. For example, TDD can ensure a strong foundation of unit tests, BDD can align the team on business requirements, and exploratory testing can uncover unexpected issues. By using these techniques in tandem, teams can achieve comprehensive test coverage and maintain high-quality standards.

Case Example

Combining TDD and BDD in a Banking Application

A banking software company used both TDD and BDD to develop a new online transaction system. TDD was employed to create robust unit tests for backend services, ensuring reliable data processing. Simultaneously, BDD scenarios were developed in Cucumber to validate user-facing features, such as account transfers and balance checks. Exploratory testing sessions uncovered usability issues that automated tests had missed, leading to an intuitive and error-free user interface. The combined approach reduced defects by 45% and accelerated delivery by 30%.

Implementing advanced Agile testing techniques like TDD, BDD, and exploratory testing enhances collaboration, improves code quality, and ensures comprehensive test coverage. By incorporating these methodologies into their workflows, Agile teams can maintain the high standards of quality required for successful project outcomes. These techniques form the foundation for integrating automation and tools, which will be explored in the next section.

Automation and Tools for Agile Testing

Automation plays a pivotal role in Agile testing, enabling teams to maintain speed and quality while managing iterative development cycles. With the right tools and strategies, Agile teams can streamline testing processes, ensure rapid feedback, and deliver high-quality software efficiently. This section explores the role of automation in Agile QA, strategies for selecting the right tools, and the integration of automated testing within Continuous Integration/Continuous Deployment (CI/CD) pipelines.

The Role of Automation in Agile QA

In Agile environments, where frequent code changes and rapid deployments are the norm, automation provides the foundation for effective and efficient testing. It supports Agile principles by accelerating feedback loops and reducing the time spent on repetitive tasks.

- **Key Benefits of Automation**:
  - **Consistency**: Automated tests ensure consistent execution, reducing human error and enabling reliable results across multiple test runs.
  - **Speed**: Automated tests run faster than manual tests, providing immediate feedback on code changes and allowing teams to address issues quickly.
  - **Scalability**: Automation enables teams to handle larger volumes of tests, ensuring thorough coverage as the codebase grows.
  - **Continuous Testing**: Automated tests integrate seamlessly into CI/CD pipelines, ensuring that tests are executed at every stage of development and deployment.

- **Areas Best Suited for Automation**:
  - **Regression Testing**: Automating regression tests ensures that new code changes do not break existing functionality.
  - **Performance Testing**: Automated tools can simulate high user loads to identify performance bottlenecks.
  - **Smoke Testing**: Quick automated checks ensure that basic functionalities are working after a new build.

Selecting the Right Tools

Choosing the right testing tools is critical to maximizing the benefits of automation. Tools should align with the project's requirements, integrate seamlessly with existing systems, and be easy for the team to adopt and maintain.

- **Criteria for Tool Selection**:
  - **Compatibility**: Ensure the tool supports the technologies used in the project (e.g., programming languages, frameworks, and platforms).
  - **Ease of Use**: Select tools with intuitive interfaces and robust documentation to reduce the learning curve for team members.
  - **Integration**: Prioritize tools that integrate with CI/CD platforms, project management tools, and other existing systems.
  - **Community and Support**: Tools with active communities and professional support ensure timely help for troubleshooting and updates.

- **Popular Automation Tools**:

  - **Selenium**: A widely used open-source framework for automating web applications, supporting multiple programming languages.

  - **Appium**: Ideal for mobile testing, Appium supports automation across iOS, Android, and Windows platforms.

  - **Cypress**: A JavaScript-based tool known for its simplicity and powerful end-to-end testing capabilities for web applications.

  - **Postman**: A versatile tool for automating API testing, allowing teams to test endpoints efficiently.

  - **JMeter**: Used for performance testing, JMeter simulates heavy user loads to identify scalability and performance issues.

Integrating Automation in CI/CD Pipelines

CI/CD pipelines are essential for Agile projects, enabling teams to integrate and deploy code changes quickly and reliably. Automation plays a central role in these pipelines, ensuring that testing keeps pace with development.

- **Continuous Integration (CI)**:

  - CI involves merging code changes frequently into a shared repository, triggering automated builds and tests. This approach identifies integration issues early, reducing the risk of defects reaching production.

  - Tools like Jenkins, GitLab CI, and CircleCI automate the execution of tests, providing immediate feedback to developers.

- **Continuous Deployment (CD)**:

  - CD extends CI by automating the deployment of tested code to staging or production environments. Automated tests act as gatekeepers, ensuring that only stable builds are deployed.

  - Deployment strategies such as blue-green deployments and canary releases can further minimize risk by introducing changes incrementally.

- **Building an Effective CI/CD Pipeline**:

  - **Setup and Configuration**: Define clear workflows for code integration, testing, and deployment. Configure triggers to execute tests automatically after code changes.

  - **Parallel Testing**: Execute multiple test suites in parallel to reduce overall testing time.

  - **Reporting and Monitoring**: Integrate tools like Allure or TestNG for detailed reporting, and use monitoring tools to track application performance post-deployment.

Challenges in Automation

While automation offers significant advantages, it also presents challenges that teams must address to maximize its effectiveness.

- **Initial Investment**: Automation requires upfront effort and resources to set up frameworks, select tools, and write test scripts. However, the long-term efficiency gains often justify the initial investment.

- **Maintenance Overhead**: Automated test scripts must be updated regularly to reflect changes in the application. A lack of maintenance can lead to false positives or negatives, reducing trust in test results.

- **Skill Gaps**: Team members may require training to use advanced automation tools effectively. Addressing these gaps through workshops and upskilling initiatives ensures successful adoption.

Case Example

Automating Testing in a Financial Services Project

A financial services company developing a new online banking platform faced challenges with maintaining quality while delivering frequent updates. By integrating automated testing into their CI/CD pipeline, the team achieved significant improvements:

- Regression tests were automated using Selenium, reducing the time spent on manual testing by 60%.

- API testing with Postman ensured reliable communication between microservices.

- Parallel test execution in Jenkins minimized feedback time, enabling faster releases. The result was a secure, high-quality platform that met stringent regulatory requirements while maintaining rapid delivery cycles.

Automation and tools are indispensable for Agile testing, supporting teams in delivering high-quality software efficiently. By selecting the right tools, integrating automation into CI/CD pipelines, and addressing common challenges, Agile teams can enhance their testing strategies and maintain the speed and quality demanded by modern development practices. This foundation sets the stage for scaling testing practices in large Agile projects, discussed in the next section.

Managing QA in Large-Scale Agile Projects

Scaling Quality Assurance (QA) in large-scale Agile projects presents unique challenges, such as maintaining consistency across multiple teams, ensuring comprehensive test coverage, and managing dependencies. This section explores strategies for effectively managing QA in large Agile projects, introduces key metrics for evaluating QA effectiveness, and discusses the integration of QA practices into Agile scaling frameworks like SAFe and LeSS.

Challenges of QA in Large-Scale Agile Projects

Large-scale Agile projects involve multiple teams working simultaneously on interdependent components. These complexities can lead to the following challenges:

- **Inconsistent Practices Across Teams**: Different teams may adopt varying QA practices, leading to inconsistencies in testing approaches and quality standards.

- **Coordination and Dependencies**: Testing interdependent features developed by different teams requires significant coordination to avoid integration issues.

- **Resource Allocation**: Ensuring that each team has adequate QA resources while managing costs can be difficult in large projects.

- **Maintaining Speed and Quality**: Scaling Agile practices can sometimes compromise speed or quality if testing is not effectively managed.

Addressing these challenges requires a combination of standardized practices, effective communication, and robust tools.

Scaling Testing Practices

To maintain quality at scale, organizations must adopt practices that promote consistency, efficiency, and collaboration across teams.

- **Establishing a Centralized QA Governance Framework**:
    - Develop a QA playbook that defines standardized processes, tools, and metrics for all teams. This ensures consistency in testing practices and simplifies reporting and evaluation.
    - Appoint QA leads or quality champions in each team to ensure adherence to the playbook and facilitate communication between teams.

- **Implementing Test Automation at Scale**:
    - Automate regression tests and other repetitive tasks to reduce manual effort and speed up testing cycles. Tools like Selenium Grid and Cypress support distributed testing, which is crucial for large-scale projects.
    - Use service virtualization tools, such as Parasoft Virtualize, to simulate dependencies between teams and test components independently.

- **Integration Testing Across Teams**:
    - Conduct regular integration testing sessions to ensure that components developed by different teams work seamlessly together. Use tools like Postman or ReadyAPI for API testing and Jenkins or GitLab CI for orchestrating integration tests in CI/CD pipelines.

- **Adopting Shift-Left Testing**:
    - Embed QA earlier in the development lifecycle by involving testers in requirements gathering, sprint planning, and design discussions. This proactive approach reduces defects and improves test coverage.

QA Metrics and Key Performance Indicators (KPIs)

To evaluate the effectiveness of QA practices in large-scale projects, organizations should track metrics that provide actionable insights into quality and process efficiency.

- **Defect Density**: Measures the number of defects per unit of code. A high defect density indicates areas of the codebase that may require refactoring or additional testing.

- **Test Coverage**: Tracks the percentage of the codebase covered by tests. Increasing test coverage ensures that critical functionality is thoroughly tested.

- **Mean Time to Detect (MTTD) and Mean Time to Resolve (MTTR)**: These metrics measure how quickly defects are identified and resolved, reflecting the efficiency of the QA process.

- **Pass/Fail Rates**: Provides insights into the stability of builds and the effectiveness of tests.

- **Release Readiness**: Combines metrics such as defect counts, test case completion rates, and stakeholder feedback to assess whether a release is ready for deployment.

Use dashboards to visualize these metrics in real-time, enabling teams and stakeholders to monitor progress and address issues promptly.

Integrating QA into Agile Scaling Frameworks

Frameworks like SAFe (Scaled Agile Framework) and LeSS (Large-Scale Scrum) provide structures for scaling Agile practices across large organizations. QA must be seamlessly integrated into these frameworks to ensure consistent quality.

- **QA in SAFe**:
  - SAFe emphasizes the importance of building quality into every aspect of development. QA is integrated into Agile Release Trains (ARTs), with dedicated testing roles within each team and a System Team responsible for system-level testing.
  - Use SAFe's concept of Built-In Quality to align QA efforts with broader organizational goals, ensuring that quality is prioritized at every level.

- **QA in LeSS**:
  - LeSS simplifies the scaling process by focusing on reducing complexity. QA responsibilities are distributed across teams, with an emphasis on cross-functional collaboration.
  - Encourage teams to share testing practices and tools, leveraging the collective knowledge of the organization to enhance QA capabilities.

Case Example

Scaling QA in a Telecom Project

A global telecom provider implementing a large-scale billing system faced challenges in coordinating QA across multiple teams. By adopting a centralized QA governance framework and leveraging automation tools, the organization achieved significant improvements:

- Introduced service virtualization tools to simulate integrations between teams, reducing delays caused by dependencies.

- Conducted bi-weekly integration testing sessions, ensuring that interdependent components functioned correctly.

- Tracked defect density and MTTD/MTTR metrics through dashboards, enabling quick identification and resolution of bottlenecks.

These practices reduced production defects by 30% and improved delivery timelines by 20%, demonstrating the value of structured QA management in large-scale Agile projects.

Managing QA in large-scale Agile projects requires a combination of standardized practices, advanced tools, and robust metrics. By scaling testing practices effectively, integrating QA into Agile frameworks, and leveraging data-driven insights, organizations can maintain high-quality standards while delivering complex projects on time. This approach ensures that even in the most challenging environments, quality remains a cornerstone of Agile success. The final part of this chapter will explore case studies and future trends in Agile QA.

Case Studies and Future Trends in Agile QA

To fully appreciate the impact of Quality Assurance (QA) in Agile environments, it's essential to examine real-world applications and explore emerging trends that are shaping the future of Agile QA. This section presents detailed case studies showcasing successful implementations of Agile QA practices and discusses future advancements, such as AI-driven testing, shift-left methodologies, and the role of QA in emerging technologies like IoT and blockchain.

Case Studies:

Real-World Applications of Agile QA

Examining real-world case studies provides actionable insights into the practical implementation of Agile QA practices and the challenges overcome during these transformations.

E-Commerce Platform

Reducing Defects Through Automation

Overview: A major e-commerce company was experiencing frequent production defects, leading to customer dissatisfaction and revenue loss during high-traffic periods.

Solution:

- The company implemented automated regression testing using Selenium and integrated these tests into its CI/CD pipeline.

- Exploratory testing sessions were conducted to uncover edge cases, particularly around payment gateway functionality.

- A defect density metric was introduced to monitor high-risk areas in the codebase.

Outcomes:

- Post-automation, the company reduced regression testing time by 70% and achieved a 40% reduction in production defects during peak seasons.

- Enhanced collaboration between developers and QA teams led to quicker identification and resolution of bottlenecks.

Financial Services

Ensuring Regulatory Compliance with BDD

Overview: A financial institution developing a new mobile banking application needed to meet stringent compliance standards while delivering a seamless user experience.

Solution:

- The team adopted Behavior-Driven Development (BDD) using Cucumber, which allowed compliance officers and developers to collaborate on feature definitions in plain language.

- Automated tests were written based on these BDD scenarios to validate compliance requirements and user flows.

- Regular sprint reviews included regulators as stakeholders to ensure alignment with legal standards.

Outcomes:

- The project achieved 100% compliance with regulatory requirements without delays.

- The use of BDD scenarios improved communication between technical and non-technical stakeholders, resulting in a user-friendly application that met customer needs.

Healthcare Network

Scaling QA in a Distributed Team

Overview: A healthcare provider deploying an integrated patient management system faced challenges in coordinating QA across distributed teams located in different time zones.

Solution:

- Service virtualization tools were used to simulate interactions between the system's components, allowing teams to test independently without waiting for dependencies.

- A centralized QA governance framework was established, with QA leads in each location coordinating efforts.

- Dashboards tracked metrics like test coverage and mean time to detect (MTTD), providing real-time visibility into progress and bottlenecks.

Outcomes:

- The project reduced integration issues by 30%, and system testing time decreased by 25% due to efficient coordination and automation.

- Enhanced visibility into QA processes helped maintain consistency and accountability across distributed teams.

Future Trends in Agile QA

The field of Agile QA is evolving rapidly, driven by technological advancements and shifting organizational priorities. The following trends are poised to shape the future of QA in Agile environments:

AI-Driven Testing

AI is transforming QA by automating complex testing tasks and providing predictive analytics to identify high-risk areas in the codebase.

- **Applications of AI in QA**:
    - **Smart Test Generation**: AI can analyze requirements and generate test cases automatically, reducing the manual effort required.
    - **Predictive Defect Detection**: Machine learning models can predict the likelihood of defects in specific areas of the application based on historical data.
    - **Self-Healing Tests**: AI-powered tools like Testim can automatically update test scripts when the application's UI changes, minimizing maintenance overhead.

Shift-Left Testing

Shift-left testing emphasizes integrating QA earlier in the development lifecycle, aligning with Agile principles of early feedback and continuous improvement.

- **Key Practices**:
    - Developers and testers collaborate on writing unit tests and acceptance criteria during sprint planning.
    - Static code analysis and security testing are performed during the development phase, reducing the cost and effort of addressing defects later.

Testing for Emerging Technologies

As technologies like IoT, blockchain, and AR/VR become more prevalent, QA practices must adapt to address their unique challenges.

- **IoT Testing**:
    - QA teams must account for hardware-software integration, scalability, and real-time data processing.
    - Tools like IoTIFY simulate IoT environments to validate functionality under different network conditions.
- **Blockchain Testing**:
    - Testing focuses on validating smart contracts, ensuring data integrity, and managing consensus mechanisms.
    - Tools like Ganache and Truffle Suite assist in automating blockchain-specific test scenarios.

- **AR/VR Testing**:
    - QA teams need to assess user experience, performance, and hardware compatibility.
    - Specialized tools like Unity Test Framework facilitate automated testing for AR/VR applications.

QA's Role in Continuous Improvement

In Agile environments, QA is not just about testing but also about driving continuous improvement across the development lifecycle.

- **Embedding QA in Retrospectives**:
    - Use retrospectives to analyze testing outcomes, identify areas for improvement, and implement process changes.

- **Data-Driven Insights**:
    - QA metrics, such as defect trends and test coverage, provide actionable insights for refining development and testing practices.

Democratization of Testing

The rise of no-code and low-code testing platforms is enabling non-technical team members, such as product owners and business analysts, to participate in QA processes.

- **Impact**:
    - Reduces the dependency on specialized QA engineers.
    - Encourages cross-functional collaboration, improving overall quality.

The integration of advanced testing practices, innovative tools, and emerging technologies ensures that Agile QA remains a dynamic and evolving discipline. By learning from real-world case studies and embracing future trends like AI-driven testing, shift-left methodologies, and IoT-specific QA practices, organizations can maintain high-quality standards while navigating increasingly complex development landscapes. QA is not merely a support function but a strategic driver of innovation and excellence in Agile projects.

Chapter 10: Scaling Agile Practices

As organizations grow and projects become more complex, the need to scale Agile practices becomes inevitable. What works seamlessly for a small team may face challenges when applied across multiple teams, departments, or even the entire enterprise. Scaling Agile is about preserving the core principles of flexibility, collaboration, and iterative delivery while adapting them to the realities of larger, more interconnected environments.

Scaling Agile practices is not simply about increasing the number of teams or projects; it requires deliberate changes in organizational structure, leadership, and processes to ensure that agility is maintained at every level. This includes addressing coordination challenges, aligning multiple teams with strategic objectives, and integrating scalable frameworks like SAFe, LeSS, or Scrum@Scale.

This chapter explores the strategies and frameworks for scaling Agile practices effectively. From understanding the challenges of scaling to implementing tools and processes that enhance collaboration and transparency, this chapter provides actionable insights for leaders. By mastering the principles of scaling Agile, organizations can achieve agility at scale, enabling them to deliver value more consistently and effectively in complex environments.

Understanding the Need for Scaling Agile

As organizations grow and projects become more complex, the straightforward Agile practices that work well in small teams may struggle to cope with increased scale. Scaling Agile involves extending the core principles of Agile—flexibility, collaboration, and continuous improvement—to larger, more complex environments. This section explores the challenges and indicators that necessitate scaling Agile practices, providing a foundation for understanding how to expand these practices effectively.

Challenges of Scaling Agile

Scaling Agile across multiple teams or departments introduces a set of unique challenges that can complicate the simplicity and directness of Agile methodologies:

- **Communication Breakdowns**: As the number of teams increases, maintaining effective communication becomes more challenging. Information silos can develop, and the alignment necessary for Agile to succeed can diminish.

- **Integration Issues**: Coordinating work across multiple Agile teams, especially when they depend on each other's outputs, can lead to integration bottlenecks. These bottlenecks can delay deliveries and reduce the overall responsiveness of the organization.

- **Consistency in Practices**: Ensuring that all teams adhere to the same Agile principles and practices is difficult when scaling. Variations in how different teams interpret and implement Agile can lead to inconsistencies in work quality and process efficiency.

- **Resource Management**: Efficiently allocating resources such as personnel, tools, and time across several Agile teams becomes more complex. Balancing resource needs without overcommitting or underutilizing becomes a critical challenge.

- **Preserving Agile Culture**: As more layers of management and more teams are added, maintaining a true Agile culture that values individual team autonomy, quick pivots based on feedback, and a flat management structure becomes increasingly difficult.

When to Scale Agile

Recognizing the right time to scale Agile practices is crucial for successful implementation. Several indicators suggest when an organization might need to consider scaling:

- **Increasing Team Sizes**: As teams grow beyond the size where everyone can communicate easily and informally (usually cited as more than 7-9 members), the need to formalize and scale Agile practices becomes apparent.

- **Multiple Interdependent Teams**: When projects span multiple teams whose outputs are interdependent, scaling Agile helps manage these dependencies more effectively.

- **Complexity in Deliverables**: As the products or services developed become more complex, involving more variables and requiring input from various specialties, scaling Agile can help manage this complexity without sacrificing agility.

- **Geographic Dispersion**: When teams are spread across different locations, whether in different offices or different countries, scaling Agile can address challenges in synchronization and communication.

- **Organizational Growth**: As an organization grows, the simple structures and processes used in small setups are often insufficient to handle increased organizational complexity effectively.

Preparing for Agile Scaling

Understanding the need to scale Agile is the first step. Preparing for this scaling involves:

- **Assessment of Current Agile Maturity**: Evaluate how well Agile methodologies are currently understood and practiced within the organization. This assessment helps determine the readiness of the organization to adopt more complex Agile scaling frameworks.

- **Strategic Planning**: Align Agile scaling initiatives with strategic organizational goals. Scaling should be driven by clear business needs and integrated into the overall strategic planning of the organization.

- **Stakeholder Buy-In**: Ensure that all levels of management and key stakeholders understand and support the move to scale Agile practices. Their buy-in is crucial for the resources and organizational backing needed to make scaling successful.

Scaling Agile is a strategic decision triggered by specific organizational needs and challenges. Understanding these challenges and the appropriate timing for scaling is crucial for preparing the organization to expand Agile practices effectively. The next parts of this chapter will explore deeper into how to implement scaling through frameworks, tools, and strategies to maintain Agile effectiveness at a larger scale.

Frameworks for Scaling Agile

As Agile methodologies have grown in popularity and proven their value in small teams, the need to scale these practices to larger groups and more complex projects has become evident. Several frameworks have been developed to address the unique challenges of scaling Agile, each offering structured guidance on how to expand Agile principles across an organization effectively. This section explores popular frameworks for scaling Agile, providing insights into their core principles, applications, and how they can be integrated into different organizational contexts.

Overview of Scaling Frameworks

Scaling Agile frameworks are designed to extend Agile principles to larger teams and complex projects that involve multiple interdependent teams. Here's a look at some of the most widely used frameworks:

- **Scaled Agile Framework (SAFe)**: SAFe is one of the most comprehensive frameworks for applying Agile practices at scale. It integrates principles from Agile, lean, and product development flow to create a scalable and modular framework suitable for enterprises. SAFe addresses all levels of an organization from team, program, to portfolio level, providing roles, responsibilities, and activities necessary for scaling.

- **Large-Scale Scrum (LeSS)**: As a simpler and more flexible approach to scaling, LeSS extends the Scrum principles to large-scale operations without adding significant complexity. LeSS focuses on de-scaling organizational complexity by minimizing roles, artifacts, and processes to achieve agility.

- **Disciplined Agile Delivery (DaD)**: DaD provides a process decision framework that enables seamless Agile adoption at an enterprise scale. It focuses on the delivery aspect of Agile projects, integrating various lifecycles including Scrum, Kanban, and more traditional processes to provide a tailored approach to Agile scaling.

- **Scrum@Scale**: Created by Jeff Sutherland, one of the original creators of Scrum, Scrum@Scale naturally extends the core Scrum framework to large enterprises by empowering networks of teams operating independently through the Scrum of Scrums approach.

Implementing a Scaling Framework

Choosing and implementing a scaling Agile framework involves several critical steps and considerations to ensure it aligns with organizational needs and enhances existing practices.

- **Assessment of Organizational Needs**: Before selecting a framework, assess the specific needs, challenges, and goals of your organization. Consider factors such as the size of the company, the complexity of projects, existing management structures, and cultural readiness for change.

- **Pilot Testing**: Start with a pilot project to implement the chosen framework on a small scale. This approach allows you to adjust and refine the framework to better suit your organization's specific conditions before wider rollout.

- **Training and Coaching**: Invest in comprehensive training and coaching for all levels of the organization. Ensure that everyone, from executives to team members, understands their roles and responsibilities within the framework and how to execute their duties effectively.

- **Continuous Evaluation and Adaptation**: Implement continuous feedback mechanisms to monitor the effectiveness of the Agile scaling initiative. Be prepared to make iterative improvements to processes, practices, and even the framework itself based on feedback and changing organizational needs.

Scaling Agile practices requires thoughtful consideration of which framework best fits an organization's unique environment. Each framework offers different emphases and tools, but all aim to preserve the core benefits of Agile—flexibility, collaboration, and efficiency—while adapting to larger and more complex project environments. The choice of framework should consider the specific challenges and goals of the organization, ensuring a custom fit that can evolve as needs change.

Building Agile Infrastructure

To effectively scale Agile practices across a large organization, it's essential to build a robust infrastructure that supports the dynamic and collaborative nature of Agile methodologies. This infrastructure includes the selection of appropriate tools and technologies, as well as the creation of support structures that foster Agile practices. This section explores the key components of Agile infrastructure necessary for scaling, highlighting how to choose tools, implement technology, and establish supportive organizational structures.

Tools and Technologies for Scaling

Scaling Agile effectively requires leveraging tools and technologies that facilitate communication, collaboration, and transparency across multiple teams and departments.

- **Project Management Software**: Tools like Jira, VersionOne, or Rally are designed to handle the complexities of large-scale Agile projects. They offer features such as backlog management, sprint planning, and progress tracking across multiple teams, enabling synchronization and coordination at scale.

- **Communication Tools**: Tools such as Slack, Microsoft Teams, or Confluence are crucial for maintaining open lines of communication and ensuring that all team members, regardless of location, are aligned and informed. These tools support instant messaging, file sharing, and real-time collaboration.

- **Continuous Integration and Continuous Deployment (CI/CD) Platforms**: Tools like Jenkins, GitLab CI, and CircleCI play a critical role in supporting Agile's emphasis on continuous delivery. They automate the process of code integration and deployment, which helps in maintaining quality and speed as the project scales.

- **Automated Testing Tools**: As projects scale, manual testing becomes impractical. Automated testing tools such as Selenium, TestComplete, and Cucumber support rapid development cycles by providing quick feedback on the impact of code changes, thus maintaining quality throughout the development process.

Creating Support Structures

Beyond tools and technologies, successful scaling of Agile practices requires the creation of organizational support structures that promote Agile values and principles.

- **Centers of Excellence (CoE)**: Establish Agile Centers of Excellence to serve as resources for best practices, guidance, and support for Agile teams across the organization. CoEs can help standardize Agile practices and offer training and mentoring to ensure consistency and effectiveness in Agile adoption.

- **Agile Coaching**: Agile coaches are critical in large-scale Agile transformations. They provide teams with the expertise needed to navigate the challenges of applying Agile practices in complex environments. Coaches help resolve process issues, guide Agile ceremonies, and ensure that Agile principles are being followed effectively.

- **Internal Agile Communities**: Foster an internal community of practice among Agile practitioners within the organization. This community can share insights, challenges, and successes from different teams, promoting a culture of learning and continuous improvement.

Integrating Agile at an Organizational Level

Scaling Agile is not just a matter of project management; it requires integrating Agile practices into the broader organizational culture and structure.

- **Alignment with Business Goals**: Ensure that Agile practices are aligned with strategic business goals. This alignment helps secure executive support and ensures that Agile transformations contribute positively to the organization's overall success.

- **Change Management**: Implement effective change management strategies to facilitate the transition to scaled Agile practices. This includes managing the cultural shift to Agile, addressing resistance, and communicating the benefits of Agile to the entire organization.

- **Scalable Architectural Practices**: Develop scalable architectural practices that support Agile development. This involves creating systems and databases that are flexible and can be easily modified or expanded as teams scale and project requirements evolve.

Building a robust Agile infrastructure is critical for successfully scaling Agile practices across large organizations. By carefully selecting tools, establishing supportive structures, and integrating Agile at an organizational level, companies can maintain the agility, responsiveness, and collaborative spirit of Agile, even in complex, multi-team environments.

Managing Culture and Communication

As organizations scale Agile practices, one of the most significant challenges they face is maintaining the Agile culture and ensuring effective communication across an expanding network of teams. This section explores strategies for preserving the core values of Agile within a large organization and enhancing communication to ensure that all team members stay aligned and engaged.

Preserving Agile Culture at Scale

Scaling Agile does not just increase the number of people involved; it also amplifies the cultural challenges. Preserving an Agile culture in a large-scale environment requires deliberate actions and policies that reinforce Agile values across all levels of the organization.

- **Leadership Involvement**: The commitment of senior leaders to Agile principles is crucial for sustaining an Agile culture as the organization grows. Leaders should actively demonstrate Agile behaviors and decision-making processes, serving as role models for the rest of the organization.

- **Cultural Artifacts**: Develop and disseminate cultural artifacts that promote and reinforce Agile values. This might include Agile manifestos, wall graphics, and regular communications that highlight stories of successful Agile practices within the organization.

- **Agile Training Programs**: Implement ongoing training programs that not only teach Agile practices but also imbue staff with the Agile mindset. These programs should be available to all employees, from new hires to upper management, to ensure a uniform understanding of Agile principles.

Effective Communication Strategies

Effective communication is the linchpin of successful Agile scaling. It bridges the gaps that physical distance and organizational layers can create in large-scale settings.

- **Scaling Communication Tools**: Utilize robust communication tools that can support large teams distributed across various locations. Tools like Microsoft Teams, Slack, or Atlassian's Confluence can facilitate instant messaging, video conferencing, and real-time document collaboration.

- **Structured Communication Cadence**: Establish a structured communication cadence that includes daily stand-ups, weekly reviews, and monthly all-hands meetings. These meetings should be carefully managed to ensure they are effective and respect participants' time. Using tools like agenda timers and designated facilitators can help keep meetings on track.

- **Visual Management Systems**: Implement visual management systems such as task boards or digital dashboards that are accessible to all team members regardless of their physical location. These systems provide a clear view of project progress, upcoming milestones, and current challenges.

Bridging Cross-Team Coordination

As organizations grow, the number of teams working on interdependent components of a project increases. Effective coordination across these teams is essential for maintaining the flow of Agile processes.

- **Integration Liaisons**: Appoint integration liaisons or Scrum Masters who specialize in coordinating efforts across teams. These individuals can help resolve dependencies, manage cross-team risks, and facilitate multi-team planning sessions.

- **Community of Practice (CoP)**: Establish communities of practice focused on different Agile roles such as Scrum Masters, Product Owners, and Agile Coaches. These communities allow members to share knowledge, discuss challenges, and develop new strategies that improve their effectiveness across teams.

- **Cross-Team Retrospectives**: Conduct cross-team retrospectives to discuss broader project challenges and opportunities for improvement. These retrospectives can help identify systemic issues that affect multiple teams and develop solutions that benefit the entire project.

Managing culture and communication effectively is key to scaling Agile practices successfully. By fostering a strong Agile culture, implementing robust communication strategies, and facilitating cross-team coordination, organizations can ensure that their Agile practices scale efficiently and effectively. This approach not only maintains the agility and responsiveness inherent in Agile but also adapts it to the complexities of large-scale operations.

Chapter 11: Leadership in High-Velocity Environments

In today's high-velocity business environments, where rapid change and uncertainty are the norm, effective leadership is more critical than ever. Agile organizations depend on leaders who can guide their teams through complexity, inspire innovation, and maintain focus on delivering value. Leadership in these environments is not about control; it's about empowerment, adaptability, and creating conditions where teams can thrive.

High-velocity environments demand a shift from traditional leadership models to a more collaborative and facilitative approach. Agile leaders must foster a culture of resilience, encourage experimentation, and ensure alignment across diverse teams and stakeholders. This requires balancing long-term vision with short-term adaptability and making decisions quickly while considering the broader impact.

This chapter examines the qualities and strategies that define effective leadership in high-velocity Agile environments. From empowering teams and managing change to navigating conflicts and fostering continuous improvement, this chapter provides actionable guidance for leaders who want to excel in fast-paced, Agile settings. By mastering these principles, leaders can drive innovation, maintain organizational alignment, and achieve sustainable success.

Characteristics of Effective Leadership in Agile

Navigating high-velocity Agile environments requires a distinctive leadership approach characterized by flexibility, foresight, and a deep commitment to fostering an Agile culture. This section explores the essential traits of effective Agile leaders, emphasizing how these characteristics influence the success and sustainability of Agile practices within an organization.

Agile Leadership Traits

Effective leadership in Agile environments goes beyond traditional management styles by emphasizing collaboration, empowerment, and continuous adaptation. Here are the key traits that define successful Agile leaders:

- **Adaptability**: Agile leaders excel in dynamic conditions, demonstrating an ability to pivot quickly in response to changing project landscapes and external factors. This adaptability involves not just adjusting strategies but also helping team members navigate the uncertainties that come with rapid change.

- **Visionary Thinking**: Agile leaders are forward-thinking, always connecting day-to-day operations with broader organizational goals. They articulate a clear vision that inspires and aligns their teams, ensuring that even the most granular tasks are linked to overarching strategic objectives.

- **Empowerment**: Central to Agile leadership is the empowerment of team members. Leaders delegate decision-making authority, foster a sense of ownership, and encourage initiative at all levels. By empowering their teams, leaders promote a more responsive, engaged, and innovative workforce.

- **Collaborative Spirit**: In contrast to top-down decision-making, Agile leaders practice and promote a collaborative approach. They facilitate open communication, encourage diverse viewpoints, and involve team members in problem-solving, thereby harnessing the collective intelligence of their teams.

- **Commitment to Learning**: A hallmark of Agile leadership is a steadfast commitment to continuous learning and improvement. Leaders foster an environment where learning from failures is as celebrated as learning from success, promoting an ongoing dialogue about improvement and innovation.

Role of Leadership in Agile Culture

Leaders significantly influence organizational culture, and in Agile environments, their impact can directly affect the agility and effectiveness of the entire organization.

- **Modeling Agile Values**: Leaders must consistently demonstrate Agile values such as responsiveness, customer focus, and teamwork. By living these values, leaders set behavioral benchmarks for the organization, embedding Agile principles deeply into the organizational fabric.

- **Creating a Supportive Environment**: Agile leaders actively work to create an environment that nurtures innovation and tolerates risk and failure. This includes providing teams with the resources they need to experiment and the freedom to fail, which are crucial for fostering a culture of innovation.

- **Encouraging Transparency**: Transparency is critical in Agile settings. Leaders encourage open discussions about challenges and successes, making it safe for team members to share their insights and concerns. This openness not only builds trust but also enhances collective problem-solving.

- **Driving Engagement**: Leaders in Agile environments engage teams by involving them in decision-making processes and recognizing their efforts and achievements. They ensure that team members feel valued and that their work is meaningful, which boosts morale and productivity.

Developing Agile Leadership Skills

The development of Agile leadership skills should be a continuous effort, involving formal training, mentoring, and practical experience.

- **Formal Training and Certification**: Leaders can benefit from formal training and certifications in Agile methodologies, which provide foundational knowledge and skills.

- **Mentoring and Coaching**: Experienced Agile coaches or mentors can help new leaders navigate their roles, offering guidance on best practices and common pitfalls.

- **Reflective Practice**: Leaders should regularly reflect on their leadership styles and decisions. This reflective practice helps them continuously refine their approaches based on feedback and outcomes, aligning more closely with Agile principles.

The characteristics and behaviors of leaders in high-velocity Agile environments are pivotal to the success of Agile practices. By embodying adaptability, visionary thinking, empowerment, collaboration, and a commitment to learning, leaders can effectively guide their teams through complexities and drive the sustained success of Agile initiatives.

Strategies for Leading Agile Teams

In Agile environments, where rapid change is the norm and teams are expected to be highly adaptive, the leadership strategy employed can significantly impact the effectiveness and morale of the team. This section explores specific strategies that leaders can use to guide and empower Agile teams, emphasizing leadership actions that foster autonomy, innovation, and alignment with Agile principles.

Empowering Agile Teams

Empowerment is a cornerstone of Agile leadership. It involves providing teams with the authority, resources, and support necessary to make decisions independently, encouraging a proactive rather than reactive approach to challenges.

- **Delegation of Decision-Making**: True empowerment requires leaders to delegate decision-making to the team members who are closest to the work. This delegation enhances the speed and appropriateness of decisions, as those making them are fully informed about the context and nuances of the situation.

- **Fostering Autonomy**: Autonomy is empowered through trust and clear boundaries. Leaders should clearly define the goals and constraints within which teams operate but leave the approach and execution to the team's discretion. This freedom encourages creative problem-solving and innovation.

- **Creating an Environment of Psychological Safety**: To truly empower teams, leaders must foster an environment where team members feel safe to express dissenting opinions, experiment with new ideas, and admit mistakes. This psychological safety is critical for driving continuous improvement and innovation.

Leading by Example

The behavior of leaders in an Agile environment sets the tone for the entire team. Leaders must not only talk the talk but also walk the walk, demonstrating Agile values and principles in their daily actions.

- **Modeling Agile Behaviors**: Leaders should model behaviors such as adaptability, continuous learning, and collaboration. By demonstrating these behaviors, leaders reinforce the Agile culture and encourage similar behaviors in team members.

- **Transparency in Leadership**: Leaders should practice transparency in decision-making and openly discuss the reasoning behind decisions, especially when they affect the team. This transparency builds trust and understanding, which are essential for effective collaboration.

- **Continuous Engagement**: Leaders should maintain a continuous presence with the team, participating in Agile ceremonies and being accessible for informal discussions. This ongoing engagement helps leaders stay connected to the team's challenges and achievements and provides opportunities for timely guidance and support.

Nurturing Growth and Development

A key responsibility of Agile leaders is to nurture the growth and development of their teams, ensuring that each member has opportunities to expand their skills and advance their careers.

- **Tailored Development Plans**: Agile leaders work with team members to develop personalized growth plans that align with their career aspirations and the needs of the team. These plans should include opportunities for training, mentorship, and rotational assignments to different roles or projects.

- **Promoting Cross-Functional Skills**: Leaders encourage team members to develop cross-functional skills that enhance team flexibility and resilience. This can involve cross-training, pair programming, or temporary role swaps within the team.

- **Recognition and Rewards**: Recognizing and rewarding contributions and achievements not only motivates team members but also reinforces the behaviors and outcomes that are valued in an Agile environment. Leaders should ensure that recognition is timely, specific, and aligned with Agile values.

Effective leadership in Agile teams involves empowering team members, leading by example, and nurturing their professional growth. These strategies ensure that teams are not only productive and innovative but also highly adaptive and aligned with the overarching goals of the organization. By implementing these leadership strategies, leaders can enhance the cohesion, morale, and performance of their Agile teams.

Navigating Challenges in High-Velocity Environments

High-velocity environments present unique challenges for leadership, including rapidly changing market conditions, high expectations for quick delivery, and the constant pressure to innovate while maintaining quality. This section explores strategies for effectively managing these challenges, ensuring that leaders can steer their teams through turbulence without sacrificing performance or well-being.

Handling Rapid Change

Agile environments are inherently dynamic, with frequent pivots and continuous adaptation being the norm. Effective leaders must not only manage this change but also use it as an opportunity to enhance team resilience and drive innovation.

- **Anticipating Change**: Leaders in high-velocity environments need to develop the ability to anticipate changes by staying informed about industry trends, technological advancements, and competitive movements. This foresight allows them to prepare their teams for impending changes, reducing the shock and disruption that sudden changes can cause.

- **Communicating Change Effectively**: When change occurs, clear and timely communication is crucial. Leaders should explain the reasons behind changes, how they align with broader organizational goals, and what they mean for individual team members. This communication should be ongoing, with regular updates as new information becomes available.

- **Flexible Planning**: While Agile emphasizes adaptability, having flexible plans that can accommodate changes without losing sight of the overall goals is vital. Leaders should foster a planning culture that allows for adjustments and refinements as projects evolve.

Conflict Resolution in Agile Teams

Conflict is inevitable in any team, especially in high-pressure, fast-paced environments. However, when managed correctly, conflict can lead to growth and improvement rather than discord.

- **Creating a Constructive Conflict Culture**: Leaders should cultivate an environment where conflicts are seen as opportunities to address problems and improve processes. This involves training team members in constructive conflict resolution techniques and encouraging open, respectful communication.

- **Mediation Skills**: Effective leaders act as mediators, helping to resolve conflicts by understanding different perspectives and finding common ground. They should be equipped with mediation skills to guide discussions, ensuring that all voices are heard and that resolutions contribute to the team's goals.

- **Preventive Measures**: By maintaining close relationships with team members and monitoring team dynamics, leaders can often anticipate and address issues before they escalate into significant conflicts.

Maintaining Team Focus and Motivation

In environments where the pace is relentless and the pressure to deliver is high, keeping teams focused and motivated is a key leadership challenge.

- **Setting Clear Goals and Priorities**: Leaders should ensure that team members understand their roles and the team's priorities. Clear goals, aligned with personal and organizational objectives, help maintain focus and drive.

- **Sustaining Engagement**: Engage team members by involving them in decision-making, recognizing their achievements, and connecting their work to the organization's success. Regular check-ins and feedback sessions can help leaders gauge morale and engagement, addressing issues as they arise.

- **Promoting Work-Life Balance**: High-velocity environments can quickly lead to burnout if not managed carefully. Leaders should promote a healthy work-life balance by setting expectations around work hours, encouraging time off, and leading by example.

Leadership in high-velocity Agile environments requires a blend of proactive change management, effective conflict resolution, and motivational skills. By anticipating and managing the challenges of rapid change, resolving conflicts constructively, and maintaining team focus and motivation, leaders can navigate their teams through complex dynamics without compromising on agility or innovation.

Building Resilience and Continuous Improvement

In high-velocity Agile environments, where rapid changes and challenges are commonplace, the ability of teams to remain resilient and continuously improve is crucial. This section explores how leaders can foster resilience among their teams and cultivate a culture of ongoing improvement to enhance performance and adaptability.

Fostering Resilience

Resilience in Agile teams is the ability to bounce back from setbacks and adapt to changes and challenges without losing momentum. Agile leaders play a critical role in building and sustaining this resilience.

- **Encouraging a Positive Response to Failure**: Leaders must create an environment where failure is seen as a learning opportunity rather than a setback. This involves openly discussing failures, analyzing them without placing blame, and encouraging a constructive response. By normalizing failure as part of the learning process, leaders help teams to take calculated risks and innovate without fear.

- **Developing Emotional Resilience**: Emotional resilience is fundamental in managing stress and uncertainty. Leaders can foster this by promoting emotional intelligence practices, such as self-awareness, self-regulation, and empathy. Workshops, training sessions, and regular team-building activities can enhance these skills, helping team members manage their emotions effectively during high-pressure situations.

- **Building Supportive Networks**: Resilient teams are underpinned by strong, supportive relationships among their members. Leaders should encourage networking within the team and across the organization to build a robust support system. This network provides a safety net that members can rely on during challenging times.

Promoting Continuous Improvement

Continuous improvement is a pillar of Agile methodologies. Effective leaders instill a mindset of ongoing development and refinement in processes, products, and skills within their teams.

- **Implementing Learning Loops**: Integrate learning loops into the team's workflows. This can be achieved through regular retrospectives where the team reflects on what has gone well and what could be improved. Action items from these sessions should be prioritized and tracked to ensure they lead to measurable improvements.

- **Leveraging Metrics and Feedback**: Use performance metrics and feedback mechanisms to guide improvements. Leaders should establish key performance indicators (KPIs) that align with team and organizational goals. Regular feedback from team members, stakeholders, and customers can also provide valuable insights into areas needing improvement.

- **Encouraging Innovation and Experimentation**: To foster an environment where continuous improvement thrives, leaders should encourage innovation and experimentation. This could mean setting aside time and resources for team members to work on innovative projects or improvements that they are passionate about, even if these are outside the usual scope of work.

Managing Knowledge and Learning

In rapidly evolving environments, the effective management of knowledge and learning is essential for maintaining a competitive edge.

- **Creating a Knowledge-Sharing Culture**: Encourage a culture where knowledge is openly shared and accessible. This might involve regular 'lunch and learn' sessions, internal wikis or databases where valuable information is stored, and encouraging mentorship programs within the team.

- **Formalizing Learning Opportunities**: Provide formal opportunities for learning and development, such as training programs, workshops, and conferences. These opportunities should not only be related to enhancing technical skills but also developing soft skills that are critical in high-velocity environments.

- **Evaluating and Adapting Training Needs**: Continuously evaluate the effectiveness of training and development programs and adapt them based on the changing needs of the team and individual members. This adaptability ensures that the team remains competent and confident in their abilities to meet new challenges.

Building resilience and fostering continuous improvement are essential for teams operating in high-velocity environments. Leaders who successfully cultivate these qualities within their teams enhance their ability to adapt to changes, overcome challenges, and continuously innovate. By focusing on resilience and continuous improvement, leaders can ensure their teams not only survive but thrive in dynamic and demanding settings.

Chapter 12: Leveraging Data and Metrics

Data and metrics are the lifeblood of modern Agile organizations, enabling informed decision-making, continuous improvement, and enhanced accountability. In an Agile environment, where adaptability and responsiveness are key, leveraging data effectively ensures that teams remain aligned with objectives, stakeholders are informed, and progress is consistently tracked.

Agile methodologies emphasize iterative delivery and real-time feedback, making data an essential tool for evaluating performance, identifying bottlenecks, and driving optimization. However, collecting data is not enough—leaders must focus on actionable metrics that provide meaningful insights without overwhelming teams with unnecessary complexity.

This chapter explores the role of data and metrics in Agile environments, covering best practices for data collection, analysis, and visualization. From tracking team performance and project progress to aligning metrics with strategic goals, this chapter provides practical tools and strategies for leveraging data effectively. By mastering these principles, leaders can create a data-driven culture that fosters transparency, accountability, and continuous improvement.

The Importance of Data in Agile Environments

In the fast-paced, iterative world of Agile software development and architecture, data plays a crucial role in guiding decisions, measuring progress, and driving improvements. This section explores the pivotal role of data in Agile decision-making, highlighting how data-driven insights can enhance transparency, increase efficiency, and foster more informed, objective decisions.

Role of Data in Agile Decision-Making

Agile methodologies emphasize the importance of adaptability and responsiveness based on continuous feedback. Data is fundamental in this context as it provides a factual basis for decisions, reducing biases and enhancing the decision-making process.

- **Enhancing Transparency**: Data collected from Agile processes (like sprint reviews, daily stand-ups, and retrospectives) provides transparent and objective insights into team performance, project progress, and potential bottlenecks. This transparency helps stakeholders and team members alike to have a clear understanding of where the project stands and what actions are needed moving forward.

- **Facilitating Predictive Decisions**: By analyzing trends from historical data, Agile leaders can anticipate issues before they become significant obstacles. Predictive analytics can help in resource allocation, sprint planning, and risk management, making the Agile process more proactive rather than reactive.

- **Improving Efficiency and Productivity**: Data allows teams to measure the effectiveness of their practices and processes quantitatively. Metrics such as velocity and cycle time give direct feedback on the team's productivity, guiding them on where they can optimize workflows and eliminate waste.

Types of Metrics Relevant to Agile Teams

Identifying and tracking the right metrics is essential for leveraging data effectively in Agile environments. Different metrics provide insights into various aspects of project health and team performance.

- **Velocity**: Measures the amount of work a team completes during a sprint and is used to gauge the team's capacity for future sprints. It helps in planning and forecasting, ensuring that commitments are realistic based on historical performance.

- **Burn-down Rates**: Burn-down charts track the amount of work remaining in a sprint or release. They are useful for visualizing progress and identifying any deviations from the planned work rate, allowing teams to adjust their strategies accordingly.

- **Lead Time and Cycle Time**: Lead time measures the total time taken from the moment a task is requested until it is fully completed. Cycle time measures the amount of time a task spends in the active workflow. Both metrics are crucial for understanding process efficiency and identifying areas where process improvements can be made.

- **Defect Density**: This metric tracks the number of defects found per unit of software size (like per functional point). It is an essential quality metric that helps teams evaluate the robustness of their coding and testing practices.

- **Customer Satisfaction**: While harder to quantify, customer satisfaction is vital. Feedback loops and surveys can measure how well the end product meets customer needs and expectations, guiding future development efforts.

Cultivating a Data-Driven Culture

Building a culture that understands and values data is critical for successful data utilization in Agile environments.

- **Education and Training**: Provide training for team members on the importance of data and metrics, how to collect and interpret them, and how they can be used to drive project decisions.

- **Data Accessibility**: Ensure that data and insights are easily accessible to all team members. Tools and dashboards should be user-friendly and provide real-time data to facilitate quick decisions.

- **Encouraging Data-Driven Decisions**: Leaders should model data-driven decision-making and reward decisions made based on solid data analysis. This encourages a shift in team culture towards valuing and utilizing data effectively.

Data is a powerful tool in the Agile toolkit, providing essential insights that drive smarter, faster, and more effective decision-making. Understanding the role of data in Agile environments and the types of metrics that can inform decision-making processes is crucial for any Agile leader looking to enhance team performance and project outcomes.

Collecting and Analyzing Agile Metrics

Effective data utilization in Agile environments is contingent upon the systematic collection and analysis of metrics. This section outlines robust techniques for gathering data and provides insights into analyzing this information to derive actionable insights that enhance project execution and management in Agile settings.

Data Collection Techniques

Efficient and accurate data collection is the bedrock of meaningful analysis and decision-making in Agile environments. Here's how leaders can ensure that their data collection methods support their strategic goals:

- **Automated Data Collection**: Utilize tools that automatically track and record key metrics from various stages of the development process. Automation reduces human error and frees up team members to focus on tasks that add more value than manual data entry.

- **Integration of Tools**: Choose tools that integrate seamlessly with each other to ensure that data flows smoothly from one platform to another. For instance, integrating project management software with version control systems and build servers can provide a holistic view of the development pipeline.

- **Real-Time Tracking**: Implement systems that offer real-time tracking capabilities to provide immediate insights into team performance, project progress, and any arising issues. Real-time data helps teams react swiftly to challenges, making adjustments before minor issues escalate.

- **Consistency in Data Collection**: Standardize the data collection process across teams to ensure consistency in the metrics collected. This standardization is crucial for comparing data across teams and over time, providing a reliable basis for analysis.

Data Analysis and Interpretation

Once data is collected, the next step is analyzing these metrics to extract meaningful insights. Proper data analysis can illuminate patterns, predict trends, and guide strategic decision-making.

- **Statistical Analysis**: Employ statistical techniques to analyze data trends and variances. For instance, use regression analysis to understand relationships between variables or time-series analysis to predict future performance based on historical data.

- **Visual Data Representation**: Convert data into visual formats such as charts, graphs, and dashboards. Visual representations make it easier to spot trends, understand complex data, and communicate findings to stakeholders who may not be familiar with raw data analysis.

- **Contextual Interpretation**: Data should be interpreted within the context of specific project goals, team dynamics, and market conditions. This contextual understanding is crucial for drawing accurate conclusions from the data and making informed decisions.

- **Actionable Insights**: Focus on extracting insights that are actionable. Data analysis should not just highlight problems but also suggest practical solutions or improvements. For instance, if cycle times are increasing, analysis should explore potential causes such as bottlenecks in the workflow and propose actionable remedies.

Feedback Loops and Continuous Improvement

Data analysis should be a cyclical process that fuels continuous improvement. Feedback loops are critical in this process:

- **Regular Review Cycles**: Establish regular intervals for reviewing collected data and the insights derived from it. These reviews can coincide with Agile ceremonies like sprint reviews or retrospectives, integrating data review into existing workflows.

- **Feedback Integration**: Encourage teams to provide feedback on the utility of the data analysis and the accuracy of the insights provided. This feedback can help refine data collection and analysis processes.

- **Iterative Adjustments**: Use insights from data analysis to make iterative adjustments to projects and processes. This continuous adjustment process aligns with Agile principles of incremental improvement and responsiveness to change.

Collecting and analyzing data in Agile environments is a dynamic, ongoing process that requires robust systems, clear methodologies, and a commitment to continuous improvement. By effectively harnessing data, Agile leaders can drive their teams and projects towards more efficient workflows, improved performance, and ultimately, greater success in their initiatives.

Implementing Data-Driven Strategies

Data-driven strategies are fundamental to maximizing the benefits of Agile methodologies in software engineering and architecture. This section explores how to integrate data insights into Agile practices, enhance productivity, improve team performance, and fine-tune processes to achieve optimal results.

Integrating Data into Agile Practices

The integration of data-driven insights into daily Agile practices helps teams become more responsive and proactive in addressing project challenges and opportunities. Here's how leaders can embed data use effectively:

- **Incorporating Data into Agile Ceremonies**: Use data collected and analyzed during daily stand-ups, sprint planning meetings, and retrospectives. For instance, velocity data can help in sprint planning by setting realistic expectations based on past performance, while retrospective data can guide improvements in processes and practices.

- **Data-Driven Sprint Reviews**: Present data-driven reports during sprint reviews that not only show what was accomplished but also provide insights into how the team can improve processes, increase efficiency, and better meet customer expectations in future sprints.

- **Real-Time Data Dashboards**: Implement real-time data dashboards that are accessible to all team members. These dashboards can display key metrics such as current sprint progress, bug counts, and build statuses, helping everyone stay informed and quickly react to issues as they arise.

Using Data to Improve Team Performance

Data is a powerful tool for identifying both strengths and areas for improvement within teams. By focusing on specific metrics, leaders can target interventions that significantly enhance team performance:

- **Performance Metrics Analysis**: Regularly analyze performance metrics like cycle times, commit-to-deploy times, and response times for customer queries. Identifying trends and outliers in these metrics can help pinpoint areas where processes can be optimized or additional training might be needed.

- **Tailored Training Programs**: Use data to develop tailored training programs that address the specific needs of the team. For example, if data shows that certain types of errors are recurring frequently, targeted training can be arranged to address these specific issues.

- **Enhancing Collaboration**: Analyze communication patterns within the team to identify potential silos or bottlenecks. Data-driven insights can lead to organizational changes that enhance collaboration, such as rearranging team structures, adjusting project management tools, or changing meeting schedules to improve synchronization.

Adapting Strategies Based on Feedback

Feedback is an integral component of the Agile process, and when combined with data, it can provide a powerful basis for adapting strategies and making informed decisions:

- **Feedback Loops**: Establish robust feedback loops that allow for the collection and analysis of feedback from all stakeholders, including team members, customers, and end-users. This feedback, alongside collected data, provides a comprehensive view of both the qualitative and quantitative aspects of project performance.

- **Data-Driven Decision Making**: Encourage decision-making processes that rely on data and feedback. For example, use A/B testing data to decide between different feature implementations based on which one performs better in terms of user engagement or satisfaction.

- **Continuous Process Adjustment**: Use insights from data and feedback to continuously adjust processes and workflows. This might involve refining estimation techniques, adjusting resource allocations, or revising development methodologies to better align with project goals and team capabilities.

Implementing data-driven strategies within Agile frameworks transforms intuition-based decisions into informed, objective actions that can significantly improve project outcomes and team performance. By systematically integrating data into Agile practices, using data to target performance improvements, and adapting strategies based on continuous feedback, leaders can ensure that their teams remain dynamic, efficient, and consistently aligned with organizational objectives.

Overcoming Challenges with Data in Agile

While leveraging data in Agile environments offers significant benefits, it also presents unique challenges. These challenges include managing the sheer volume of data, ensuring data relevance and accuracy, and maintaining privacy and security. This section explores strategies to address these challenges effectively, ensuring that data utilization enhances rather than hinders Agile processes.

Addressing Data Overload

The abundance of data available can lead to overload, where the sheer volume makes it difficult to discern what data is valuable and what is not. Here's how leaders can manage this challenge:

- **Selective Data Tracking**: Instead of trying to capture and analyze every piece of data, leaders should focus on metrics that directly impact key performance indicators (KPIs) and organizational goals. This selective approach prevents data fatigue and keeps teams focused on actionable insights.

- **Data Prioritization**: Implement systems to prioritize data based on its potential impact on decision-making. Use techniques such as weighted scoring or impact analysis to help teams focus on high-priority data that offers the most significant insights.

- **Streamlining Data Sources**: Consolidate data sources to reduce complexity and overlap. This not only simplifies data management but also enhances the quality of insights by reducing discrepancies between data sets.

Ensuring Data Privacy and Security

In the age of data breaches and stringent data privacy regulations, ensuring the security and privacy of data used in Agile processes is paramount. Here's how Agile leaders can tackle these concerns:

- **Implement Robust Security Protocols**: Adopt comprehensive data security measures, including encryption, secure access controls, and regular security audits. Ensure that all tools and technologies used for data collection and analysis comply with industry standards for data security.

- **Privacy by Design**: Incorporate privacy considerations into the development process from the outset. This involves understanding the data privacy laws applicable to the organization and ensuring all data handling practices are compliant.

- **Regular Training on Data Security**: Conduct regular training sessions for all team members on best practices for data security and privacy. This helps foster a culture of security awareness and ensures everyone understands their role in protecting sensitive information.

Managing Data Accuracy and Relevance

Data-driven decisions are only as good as the data they are based on. Ensuring data accuracy and relevance is crucial for effective decision-making.

- **Regular Data Validation**: Implement processes for regular validation and cleansing of data to ensure it remains accurate and reliable. This may involve routine audits of data sources, automated error checking, and procedures for quickly correcting identified data issues.

- **Feedback Mechanisms for Data Quality**: Establish feedback mechanisms that allow team members to report inaccuracies or anomalies in the data they work with. This not only helps maintain data integrity but also engages the team in ongoing quality assurance.

- **Adapting Data Strategies to Project Evolution**: Agile projects are dynamic, with changing needs and goals. Regularly review and adapt data collection and analysis strategies to align with the current state of the project. This ensures that the data remains relevant and provides valuable insights throughout the project lifecycle.

Effectively managing the challenges associated with data in Agile environments is essential for harnessing the full potential of data-driven strategies. By addressing data overload, ensuring data privacy and security, and maintaining data accuracy and relevance, Agile leaders can enhance decision-making processes, improve project outcomes, and ensure compliance with regulatory requirements. These strategies not only mitigate potential risks but also maximize the strategic value of data within Agile frameworks.

Chapter 13: Innovative Technologies and Future Trends

The world of software engineering and architecture is continuously evolving, driven by groundbreaking innovations and shifting technological landscapes. For Agile organizations, staying ahead of these changes requires not only embracing emerging technologies but also understanding how they intersect with Agile principles. As technologies like AI, blockchain, IoT, and quantum computing reshape industries, Agile leaders must prepare their teams to harness these advancements effectively.

Innovative technologies present opportunities to enhance agility, streamline workflows, and deliver greater value to customers. However, they also introduce new challenges, including ethical considerations, complexity in testing and deployment, and the need for continuous learning. Addressing these challenges requires a forward-thinking mindset and strategies that align technological innovation with organizational goals.

This chapter explores the intersection of Agile practices with emerging technologies and future trends. From integrating new tools and frameworks to preparing teams for shifts in the technological landscape, this chapter provides insights into navigating the future of software engineering and architecture. By staying informed and adaptable, Agile organizations can leverage innovation to drive growth, resilience, and competitive advantage.

Overview of Emerging Technologies

The rapid pace of technological innovation continues to transform the landscape of software engineering and architecture. Agile environments, known for their flexibility and responsiveness, are particularly well-suited to integrate and capitalize on these advances. This section provides an overview of current technological innovations that are reshaping the industry and examines their impact on Agile practices.

Current Technological Innovations

In the realm of software engineering and architecture, several key technologies are making significant impacts and promise to drive future developments:

- **Artificial Intelligence and Machine Learning**: AI and ML are revolutionizing the way software is developed, tested, and deployed. These technologies enable more intelligent automation, predictive analytics, and enhanced decision-making processes, making Agile teams more efficient and proactive.

- **Internet of Things (IoT)**: IoT technology connects billions of devices, generating vast amounts of data that can be used to enhance decision-making and create more responsive, user-centered software solutions. For Agile teams, this means an increased focus on integrating and managing IoT-driven data for real-time application updates and enhancements.

- **Blockchain**: Known primarily for its role in cryptocurrency, blockchain technology offers significant advantages in terms of security and data integrity. Its applications in software architecture include secure transaction management and enhanced data privacy, which are critical in sectors like finance and healthcare.

- **Cloud Computing**: As cloud technology continues to evolve, it offers Agile teams scalable infrastructure that can adjust quickly to changing needs without the upfront cost of traditional hardware. The cloud supports Agile practices by facilitating collaboration, remote working, and continuous delivery.

- **Augmented Reality (AR) and Virtual Reality (VR)**: AR and VR technologies are creating new frontiers in user interfaces. Software teams are increasingly tasked with integrating these technologies into applications, ranging from immersive training platforms to enhanced customer service experiences.

Impact on Agile Practices

The integration of these technologies into Agile environments not only enhances capabilities but also presents new challenges and opportunities for Agile practices:

- **Enhanced Automation and Efficiency**: AI and ML can automate complex tasks that were previously manual, such as data analysis, testing, and even some aspects of coding. This automation allows Agile teams to focus more on innovation and less on routine tasks.

- **Data-Driven Decision Making**: With technologies like IoT and blockchain, teams have access to real-time, accurate data that can inform decisions throughout the Agile process. This capability enables more responsive and adaptive project management.

- **New Skill Requirements**: As new technologies emerge, Agile teams must adapt by acquiring new skills. This ongoing learning is crucial to remain competitive and effective in implementing state-of-the-art solutions.

- **Collaboration Across Disciplines**: Emerging technologies often require a blend of skills from different disciplines. Agile teams must enhance their collaboration tools and practices to integrate diverse expertise effectively.

Cultivating a Tech-Forward Agile Culture

To successfully integrate these technologies, Agile leaders must foster a culture that not only embraces change but also actively seeks to understand and experiment with emerging trends.

- **Continuous Learning and Adaptation**: Encourage an organizational culture that values continuous learning. Provide training and development opportunities focused on emerging technologies and encourage experimentation.

- **Strategic Partnerships**: Establish partnerships with tech firms and educational institutions to stay ahead of technology trends and gain early access to innovations.

- **Feedback and Iteration**: Utilize feedback mechanisms to gauge the effectiveness of technology integration and continuously iterate on technology strategies based on real-world use and outcomes.

The dynamic interplay between emerging technologies and Agile practices offers exciting opportunities to redefine the boundaries of software engineering and architecture. By understanding these technologies and their potential impacts, Agile leaders can strategically position their teams to take full advantage of technological advancements.

Integrating New Technologies into Agile Environments

As Agile environments continually evolve, integrating new technologies becomes imperative for maintaining competitiveness and driving innovation. This section outlines strategies for adapting Agile frameworks to incorporate emerging technologies effectively, ensuring that these integrations enhance rather than disrupt Agile processes.

Adapting Agile Frameworks to New Technologies

Agile frameworks are inherently adaptable but require thoughtful modification to accommodate new technologies seamlessly. Here are strategies to ensure that emerging technologies are integrated effectively into Agile practices:

- **Incremental Integration**: Adopt an incremental approach to integrating new technologies, similar to how software features are rolled out in Agile projects. This method allows teams to manage risks associated with new technologies by testing their impact in controlled stages and adjusting the integration process based on feedback and results.

- **Customizing Agile Ceremonies**: Modify Agile ceremonies to include specific discussions and planning around new technologies. For instance, during sprint planning, allocate time to discuss how new tools like AI-based analytics can be used to optimize tasks. Similarly, in retrospectives, evaluate the effectiveness of these technologies in meeting project goals.

- **Updating User Stories and Backlogs**: Incorporate requirements and tasks specific to new technologies into user stories and product backlogs. This integration ensures that the adoption of technologies like IoT or blockchain is aligned with the project's overall objectives and delivers real user value.

Training and Skill Development

The rapid pace of technological change necessitates continuous learning and skill development within Agile teams. Here's how organizations can support their teams in staying up-to-date with new technologies:

- **Targeted Training Programs**: Develop and implement training programs that are specifically tailored to the technologies being adopted. For instance, if a team is integrating AI and machine learning, provide access to courses and workshops that cover these areas in depth.

- **Learning and Development Plans**: Include technology training as a key component of personal development plans. Encourage team members to set learning goals related to new technologies and support these goals with resources and time for education.

- **Cross-Functional Training**: Encourage team members to learn about roles and perspectives other than their own, particularly in contexts where new technologies blur the lines between traditional roles (e.g., developers needing to understand data science elements in AI projects).

Leveraging Expertise

Incorporating new technologies often requires expertise that may not exist within the current team. Here are strategies to access and integrate this needed expertise:

- **Hiring Specialists**: When necessary, hire new team members who bring specific technological expertise. These specialists can accelerate the learning curve for existing teams and help embed new technologies more effectively.

- **Consultants and Partnerships**: Engage with consultants or form partnerships with technology providers who can offer specialized knowledge and insights. This approach not only brings in expertise but also helps in navigating the complexities associated with implementing cutting-edge technologies.

- **Community Engagement**: Encourage team members to participate in technology communities and forums. These platforms can provide valuable insights and peer support for navigating challenges associated with new technologies.

Integrating new technologies into Agile environments requires careful planning, targeted training, and strategic use of external expertise. By methodically adapting Agile practices to accommodate these technologies, organizations can enhance their capabilities and remain competitive in an ever-evolving digital landscape. Effective integration leads to teams that are not only proficient in using new tools but also excel in leveraging them to deliver innovative, high-quality products and services.

Future Trends in Software Engineering and Architecture

The field of software engineering and architecture is perpetually evolving, driven by technological advances and shifts in business and consumer expectations. This section explores predicted future trends that are likely to influence the industry significantly, offering insights on how Agile leaders can prepare their teams for these impending changes.

Predictions for Future Developments

Understanding future trends is crucial for staying ahead in the highly competitive tech industry. Here are several key developments that Agile leaders need to watch:

- **Increased Emphasis on Artificial Intelligence and Automation**: AI is expected to become even more integral to software development processes, automating tasks ranging from code generation to testing and deployment. This shift will likely change the roles and skills required within Agile teams and could lead to more efficient development cycles.

- **Rise of Quantum Computing**: As quantum computing moves from experimental to more practical applications, it will begin to solve problems beyond the reach of classical computers, especially in fields like cryptography, optimization, and simulation. Software teams will need to understand quantum algorithms and their implications on existing software solutions.

- **Pervasive Use of IoT**: IoT technology will continue to expand into new industries, creating more interconnected environments. This expansion will require Agile teams to integrate and manage a greater number of devices and data streams, emphasizing the need for robust cybersecurity measures.

- **Progress in Edge Computing**: With the growth of IoT devices, edge computing will become more important. It processes data near the source to improve response times and save bandwidth. Agile teams will need to adapt their development practices to create and manage software that runs effectively in distributed environments.

- **Evolution of 5G**: The rollout of 5G technology is set to accelerate, enhancing mobile connectivity and enabling the high-speed, real-time data transfer needed for technologies like AR and VR. Agile teams will be challenged to develop applications that leverage the ultra-low latency and high speeds of 5G.

- **Advancements in Blockchain**: Beyond its financial applications, blockchain technology is poised to enhance software solutions in areas such as supply chain, healthcare, and public records due to its security and transparency features. Agile teams will need to integrate blockchain to capitalize on these benefits.

Preparing for Future Challenges

To stay relevant and effective, Agile teams must adapt to these technological advancements and prepare for the challenges they bring:

- **Fostering a Culture of Continuous Learning**: Encourage a learning environment where ongoing education and skill development are prioritized. Invest in training programs and resources that allow team members to stay abreast of new technologies and methodologies.

- **Agile Adaptation to New Technologies**: Agile frameworks may need to be adjusted to accommodate new types of work or workflows introduced by emerging technologies. For example, the integration of AI might require changes in sprint planning and review processes to include AI behavior evaluations.

- **Strategic Innovation Initiatives**: Establish innovation labs or dedicated teams that focus on experimenting with and understanding new technologies. These groups can explore innovative applications and assess the impact of these technologies on current projects.

- **Enhanced Collaboration Tools**: As projects incorporate more advanced technologies, the need for sophisticated collaboration tools will increase. Investing in advanced project management and communication tools will be crucial for coordinating efforts across increasingly specialized and distributed teams.

The future of software engineering and architecture is marked by rapid and continuous change. For Agile leaders, staying informed about these trends is just the start. They must proactively prepare their teams through education, adaptive practices, and strategic investments in technology. By doing so, they can ensure their teams not only adapt to but also thrive in the future landscape of software development.

Ethical Considerations and Sustainable Practices

As technology advances rapidly and becomes more integrated into every aspect of our lives, the ethical implications and the sustainability of these technologies take on critical importance. This section discusses the ethical challenges and sustainability concerns associated with new technologies in software engineering and architecture, and how Agile teams can address these issues responsibly.

Navigating Ethical Implications

The integration of emerging technologies into software products often raises complex ethical questions, particularly related to privacy, security, and equity. Agile leaders must ensure that their teams are not only aware of these issues but also equipped to address them in their projects.

- **Data Privacy and Security**: As technologies like AI and IoT collect and process vast amounts of personal data, ensuring the privacy and security of this data becomes paramount. Agile teams must incorporate privacy by design and follow best practices for data security, regularly updating their methods in response to new threats.

- **Bias and Fairness in AI**: AI systems can inadvertently perpetuate or even exacerbate biases if not carefully designed and tested. Agile leaders should ensure that their teams are trained to recognize and mitigate biases in AI algorithms and datasets. This involves diverse team compositions, rigorous testing scenarios, and transparency in AI decision-making processes.

- **Accountability**: As systems become more autonomous, determining accountability for decisions made by AI becomes challenging. Agile teams must define clear guidelines for accountability, ensuring that human oversight is maintained in critical decision-making processes and that systems are auditable and explainable.

Emphasizing Sustainability

Sustainability in software engineering extends beyond environmental considerations to include the long-term viability and maintenance of software solutions. Here's how Agile teams can promote sustainability:

- **Resource Efficiency**: Encourage practices that reduce the resource footprint of software solutions, such as optimizing code for energy efficiency and selecting technologies that reduce the overall energy consumption of the end products.

- **Sustainable Development Practices**: Adopt development practices that consider the environmental impact of software projects. This could include using green data centers, recycling hardware, and minimizing waste during the development process.

- **Lifecycle Management**: Focus on creating software that is not only robust and maintainable but also adaptable to future changes, reducing the need for frequent replacements and the associated environmental impact.

- **Promoting Ethical Standards**: Develop and enforce ethical standards and guidelines that address both the immediate and long-term impacts of software projects. This includes considering the societal impacts of deployments and ensuring that projects contribute positively to the communities they affect.

Implementing Ethical and Sustainable Practices

Implementing ethical and sustainable practices requires a strategic approach and commitment at all levels of the organization:

116

- **Ethics and Sustainability Training**: Provide regular training for team members on the latest ethical and sustainability issues in technology. This training should include practical guidelines on how to address these issues in day-to-day work.

- **Stakeholder Engagement**: Involve stakeholders, including customers, community representatives, and industry experts, in discussions about ethical and sustainability issues. This engagement can provide valuable insights and help ensure that projects meet broader social and environmental standards.

- **Monitoring and Reporting**: Establish mechanisms for monitoring the ethical and environmental impact of projects and for reporting these impacts to stakeholders. Transparency in these areas not only builds trust but also encourages continuous improvement.

Ethical considerations and sustainable practices are increasingly becoming critical components of software engineering and architecture. By proactively addressing these issues, Agile leaders can guide their teams to not only develop innovative technologies but also ensure that these technologies are responsible and sustainable, thereby contributing to a more ethical and sustainable future.

Conclusion:

Embracing Agile Leadership for Future Challenges

As we conclude "Executive Strategies for Agile Software Engineering and Architecture," we reflect on the comprehensive journey through the multifaceted landscape of Agile practices, from foundational principles and methodologies to the integration of cutting-edge technologies and ethical considerations. This book has navigated through the core aspects of Agile leadership, underscoring the pivotal role that adaptive, responsive, and forward-thinking management plays in the success of software engineering and architecture projects.

Key Takeaways

1. **Agile Foundations**: Understanding the essence of Agile—its principles, practices, and methodologies—is crucial for any leader seeking to implement or improve Agile strategies within their organization. We've explored how Agile's flexibility, emphasis on collaboration, and focus on continuous delivery are instrumental in driving project success.

2. **Leadership in Agile**: Effective Agile leadership is not just about managing processes; it's about inspiring and guiding people. Leaders in Agile environments must embody and promote Agile values, empower their teams, facilitate continuous learning, and adapt leadership styles to meet the evolving needs of their projects and teams.

3. **Technological Integration**: As technology continues to evolve at a rapid pace, integrating new tools and technologies into Agile frameworks is essential. Leaders must stay informed about technological advancements, understand their implications, and ensure their teams are equipped to leverage these innovations effectively.

4. **Data-Driven Agility**: Leveraging data and metrics enhances decision-making and operational efficiency in Agile environments. We've discussed how leaders can effectively gather, analyze, and utilize data to optimize processes, predict trends, and make informed strategic decisions.

5. **Ethical and Sustainable Practices**: The future of Agile software engineering must also consider the ethical implications and sustainability of technological solutions. Leaders are tasked with ensuring that their practices not only comply with ethical standards but also contribute positively to societal and environmental well-being.

Preparing for the Future

The landscape of software engineering and architecture is perpetually changing, driven by innovations and shifts in the global business environment. Agile leaders must therefore cultivate an environment of continual learning and adaptation. By embracing the strategies discussed in this book, leaders can prepare their teams for future challenges, ensuring resilience and continued success in an increasingly complex world.

Leaders are encouraged to view this book not just as a collection of strategies but as a catalyst for transformation within their own organizations. Implementing the principles and practices outlined here requires commitment, courage, and a proactive approach to leadership and change management.

As you move forward, keep revisiting the concepts and strategies discussed, adapting them to your unique circumstances and evolving them as you gain more insights and experiences. The journey of Agile is continuous, and your leadership will be the cornerstone of your organization's success in navigating this journey.

With this conclusion, we encapsulate the essence of Agile leadership and its critical role in shaping the future of software engineering and architecture. As the Agile landscape evolves, so too should the strategies and approaches of those who lead it, ensuring that they remain not only relevant but also instrumental in achieving excellence and innovation.

References:

Scrum.org. *"The Scrum Guide: The Definitive Guide to Scrum"*.

SAFe. *"Scaled Agile Framework Implementation Roadmap"*.

LeSS. *"The LeSS Framework Overview."* Large-Scale Scrum Organization

Atlassian. *"Agile with Jira Software: A Guide to Agile Development."*

Jenkins Documentation. *"Continuous Integration Best Practices."*

SeleniumHQ. *"Selenium Testing Tools and Frameworks Guide."*

ISO/IEC 25010: *"System and Software Quality Models."*

IEEE 1471-2000: *"Recommended Practice for Architectural Description of Software-Intensive Systems."*

Notes: